The French
Country Table

RYLAND
PETERS
& SMALL

LONDON NEW YORK

The French Country Table

Simple recipes for bistro classics

Laura Washburn with photography by Martin Brigdale

Design and Photographic Art Direction
Steve Painter
Senior Commissioning Editor Julia Charles
Production Maria Petalidou
Art Director Leslie Harrington
Publishing Director Alison Starling

Food Stylists Linda Tubby and Bridget Sargeson
Prop Stylist Helen Trent
Indexer Hilary Bird

First published in the US in 2010
by Ryland Peters & Small, Inc.
519 Broadway, 5th Floor
New York, NY 10012
www.rylandpeters.com

10 9 8 7 6 5 4 3 2 1

Printed in China

Library of Congress Cataloging-in-Publication
Data

Washburn, Laura.
   The French country table : simple recipes for
bistro classics / Laura Washburn ; with
photography by Martin Brigdale.
     p. cm.
   Includes index.
   ISBN 978-1-84975-023-3
   1. Cookery, French. I. Brigdale, Martin. II. Title.
   TX719.W3398 2010
   641.5944--dc22
                                    2010017577

The recipes in this book have been published
previously by Ryland Peters & Small in *Bistro*
and *French Desserts*.

Notes
• All spoon measurements are level, unless
otherwise specified.
• All herbs are fresh unless specified as dried.
• All eggs are large, unless otherwise specified. It
is generally recommended that free-range eggs
be used. Uncooked or partially cooked eggs should
not be served to the very young, the very old,
those with compromised immune systems, or
to pregnant women.
• When a recipe calls for the grated peel of citrus
fruit, buy unwaxed fruit and wash well before
using. If you can only find treated fruit, scrub well
in warm soapy water and rinse before using.
• Ovens should be preheated to the specified
temperature. Recipes in this book were tested
using a regular oven. If using a fan-assisted oven,
follow the manufacturer's instructions for adjusting
temperatures. However, as a general rule fan-oven
temperatures should be reduced by about 10°F
for every 100°F and cooking times reduced by
10 minutes for each hour above the first hour.

Contents

Introduction

The cuisine of France is exceptional. It is based on local ingredients and regional recipes, and a great deal of respect for tradition. Many of the ingredients in French cuisine can be found most anywhere in the world: garden-fresh vegetables like green beans, tomatoes, potatoes, and herbs; poultry, lamb, and beef are prominent; the coastlines offer an abundance of seafood, and the tradition of French cheese-making is world renowned. So what is it they do with these kitchen basics that makes their cuisine stand out from the rest?

One essential ingredient is simplicity. French cuisine suffers from a misconception that it is complicated, but the best French food is inherently straightforward. 'Faites simple' (keep it simple) is the advice given centuries ago by one of the greatest French chefs of all time, Auguste Escoffier. To my mind, this represents the essence of French cuisine. It's not elaborate, it's everyday food for ordinary people.

Another vital component is time. The French take time for food. They take time to produce it, to shop for it and to prepare it but, mostly, they take the time to eat it. And this is one thing we all have. Even in a busy world, even on a budget, time is there for the taking.

The collection of recipes in this book is a testament to the glory of French food, in all its simplicity. Nothing fancy, nothing complicated. And if you feel pressed for time in this busy world, think again. Simple food is often fast food.

The recipes in this book are also a collection of memories, of the things that made life different and special when I lived in France. Not only did I learn to cook there, I learned to enjoy food. And I came to appreciate the rituals around food: the transferring of family recipes from one generation to the next, shopping at the market, and spending most of Sunday afternoon eating lunch.

When I think back, the most pleasurable experience occurred before I even got into the kitchen; I loved shopping for food. Of course, we bought items at the supermarket, but this was usually basics and staples. The important things were bought at the market, or from speciality shops like cheese from the fromager, fresh bread from the boulangerie, or sausage from the traiteur.

After I finished cooking school, I began to work for Patricia Wells. At the time, she lived near one of Paris's best street markets, which meant I had the good fortune of passing through each day on the way home, with a head full of ideas for dinner after a day spent researching, editing, and translating recipes. I got to know the people who sold me the food, often by name, and they got to know my preferences. When truffle season started, Monsieur Claude from the traiteur shop always made sure to keep one very small truffle just for me. And he taught me that if I kept it for a few weeks in an a well-sealed jar of very good short-grain rice (which he also sold me!), the rice would take on the flavors and I could use it for truffle-scented risotto.

I've always liked to eat, but France taught me to love food. I learned to respect the quality of ingredients, and the skill of the people who produce such things, and I discovered that where something was grown, and even how, mattered. I loved the way each day there was constructed around a meal as if nothing else could possibly be more important than food.

Fortunately, the pleasure of cooking and eating like I did in France is a memory I can keep alive, and share, no matter where in the world I am.

Appetizers

Rustic pâté with green peppercorns

Terrine de campagne au poivre vert

If you've never made your own terrine, try this. It is simplicity itself, and you may never use store-bought pâtés again. If you ask your butcher to grind all the meat, except the liver, then it will be even easier. Serve in slices to begin an informal meal, with plenty of fresh baguette, unsalted butter, and French cornichons. It also makes a great sandwich filling.

1 lb. boneless pork shoulder (fat not trimmed), ground

1 lb. veal, ground

8 oz. calves' liver, finely chopped

1 egg, beaten

2 shallots, finely chopped

2 garlic cloves, crushed

1 tablespoon coarse sea salt

freshly ground black pepper

2 tablespoons green peppercorns in brine, drained, plus extra for decorating

½ teaspoon ground allspice

3 tablespoons Cognac

a handful of fresh bay leaves (see method)

To serve

French cornichons
unsalted butter
sliced baguette

a rectangular terrine mold, 12 x 14 inches

parchment paper

Serves 10–12

Preheat the oven to 350°F.

Put the pork, veal, and liver in a large bowl. Add the egg, shallots, garlic, salt, pepper, green peppercorns, allspice, and Cognac and mix well, preferably with your hands.

Fill the mold with the meat mixture, patting to spread evenly. Arrange the bay leaves on top of the mold and dot with extra green peppercorns. Set it in a roasting pan and add enough boiling water to come half-way up the sides of the mold. Cover the terrine with foil and bake in the preheated oven for about 1½ hours, until a knife inserted in the middle is hot to the touch after 30 seconds.

Remove from the oven and let cool. When the terrine is at room temperature, cover with parchment paper and weight with a few food cans. Refrigerate, with the weights on top. Leave for at least 1 day, but 3 days is best. The pâté will keep, refrigerated, for 1 week. Bring to room temperature before serving.

Mackerel pâté Rillettes de maquereaux

Rillettes, a coarse but spreadable pâté, is normally made from pork or goose. This is a lighter version, made from mackerel poached in white wine, giving it a pleasant, almost pickled taste. Serve this straight from the bowl, passing it around the table at the start of an informal gathering, or spread it on crackers and serve with drinks. There's no point making this in small batches—but it freezes well, in case this is more than you need, or if you have leftovers.

2 fresh mackerel, about 14 oz. each, well cleaned, with heads on

1 onion, sliced

3 tablespoons unsalted butter, cut into pieces and melted or softened

a large handful of flat-leaf parsley

a few sprigs of tarragon, leaves stripped

freshly squeezed juice of 1 lemon

a dash of Tabasco

coarse sea salt and freshly ground black pepper

Court bouillon

1 carrot, sliced

1 onion, sliced

1 lemon, sliced

1 sprig of thyme

1 fresh bay leaf

a few black peppercorns

1 clove

750-ml bottle dry white wine

2 teaspoons salt

To serve

toast or sliced baguette

lemon wedges

Serves 6—8

One day before serving, put all the court bouillon ingredients in a saucepan. Bring to a boil over high heat, boil for 1 minute, then cover and simmer gently for 20 minutes.

Preheat the oven to 300°F. Make 3 slits in the mackerels on either side, to help the flavors to penetrate the flesh. Put them in a large baking dish and pour over the hot court bouillon. Cook in the preheated oven for 30 minutes. Let cool in the liquid, then cover and refrigerate overnight.

The day of serving, remove the mackerel from the dish and lift the fillets, removing as many bones as possible.

Put the fillets, and most of the onion, in a food processor. Add the butter, parsley, and tarragon and blend briefly. Transfer to a serving bowl and stir in the lemon juice, Tabasco, and a generous grinding of pepper. Taste and adjust the seasoning.

Refrigerate until firm, then serve with toast or sliced baguette and lemon wedges for squeezing.

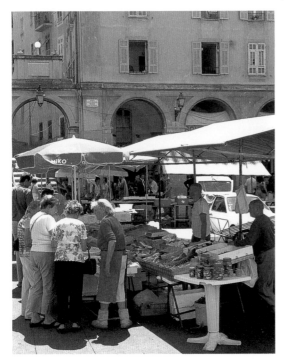

On a visit to France, we went to the elegant seaside town of Hossegor. We window-shopped around the center, then strolled through the back streets, trying to choose which villa we would buy when we won the lottery. By the time we got to the seafront, we were famished. The first restaurant we saw had chipirons à l'ail written on the blackboard so we sat down, ordered some, and had a most memorable meal. Chipirons are tiny squid, very sweet and delicate, and unavailable where I live, but shrimp are a good substitute. Serve with lots of bread to mop up the garlicky sauce.

Garlic prawns Crevettes à l'ail

½ cup olive oil

2 lbs. shrimp tails, with shells

8–10 garlic cloves, chopped

a large handful of flat-leaf parsley, chopped

coarse sea salt and freshly ground black pepper

lemon wedges, to serve

Serves 4

Heat the oil in a large sauté pan. When hot but not smoking, add the shrimp and garlic and cook for 3–5 minutes, until the shrimp turn pink. Be careful not to let the garlic burn.

Remove from the heat, sprinkle with salt, freshly ground black pepper, and parsley and mix well. Serve immediately, with plenty of lemon wedges on the side for squeezing.

Crudités

Crudités are a classic appetizer, especially in Parisian cafés and bistros, and they are a favorite of mine. The combination of ingredients given is fairly representative, but it does vary. Canned corn and tuna are common, as are hard-cooked eggs. You could quite easily make a meal of this by increasing the quantities or adding other ingredients to make it more elegant and contemporary. Try quail's eggs, sliced cherry tomatoes, peeled blanched fava beans or wafer-thin red onion slices.

2 tablespoons wine vinegar

¼ red cabbage, thinly sliced

8 oz. baby new potatoes

7 oz. fresh asparagus spears or haricots verts

3 medium carrots, grated

1 tablespoon freshly squeezed lemon juice

3 cooked beets

1 medium cucumber

a handful of flat-leaf parsley, finely chopped

fine sea salt

1 baguette, sliced, to serve

Vinaigrette

3 tablespoons wine vinegar

1 teaspoon fine sea salt

2 teaspoons Dijon mustard

10 tablespoons safflower oil

freshly ground black pepper

Serves 4

To make the vinaigrette, put the vinegar in a bowl. Using a fork or a small whisk, stir in the salt until almost dissolved. Mix in the mustard until completely blended. Add the oil, 1 tablespoon at a time, whisking well between each addition, until emulsified. Add pepper to taste. Set aside.

Heat the vinegar in a saucepan. As soon as it reaches a boil, remove from the heat, add the red cabbage and toss well. Salt lightly and set aside until the cabbage turns an even deep, fuchsia color.

Meanwhile, put the potatoes in a saucepan with sufficient cold water to cover. Bring to a boil, add salt, and cook for about 15 minutes, until tender. Drain, peel, and slice thinly.

Bring another saucepan of water to a boil. Add the asparagus and cook for 3–5 minutes, until just tender. Drain and set aside.

Put the carrots, lemon juice, and a pinch of salt in a bowl and toss well; set aside. Cut the beets in quarters lengthwise, then slice thinly to get small triangular pieces. Peel the cucumber, cut it in quarters lengthwise and slice.

Arrange small mounds of each ingredient on plates, alternating colors. Add a few spoonfuls of vinaigrette to each one and sprinkle with parsley. Serve with a basket of sliced baguette.

Goat cheese tart — Tarte au chèvre

Unlike most dishes cooked with cheese, this is very light and elegant, perfect to serve before a rich stew. It is also very moreish and you could be tempted to make a meal of it with a simple green salad. Alternatively, you could make individual tarts for a picnic, buffet or dinner party. Serve with a white wine from the Loire.

1½ cups all-purpose flour, plus extra for rolling

7 tablespoons cold unsalted butter, cut into pieces

a pinch of salt

3–4 tablespoons cold water

Goat cheese filling

3 eggs

1 cup crème fraîche or sour cream

3 Crottin de Chavignol goat cheeses, about 2–3 oz. each

2 oz. Gruyère cheese, finely grated

a small bunch of chives, snipped

fine sea salt

parchment paper and baking weights or dried beans

a loose-based tart pan, 11 inches diameter

Serves 4—6

To make the pastry, put the flour, butter, and salt in a food processor and, using the pulse button, process until the butter is broken down (about 5–10 pulses). Add 3 tablespoons cold water and pulse just until the mixture forms coarse crumbs; add 1 more tablespoon if necessary, but do not do more than 10 pulses.

Transfer the pastry to a sheet of parchment paper, form into a ball and flatten to a disk. Wrap in parchment paper and refrigerate for 30–60 minutes.

Roll out the pastry on a floured work surface to a disk slightly larger than the tart pan. Carefully transfer the pastry to the pan, patching any holes as you go and pressing gently into the sides. To trim the edges, roll a rolling pin over the top, using the edge of the pan as a cutting surface and let the excess fall away. Tidy up the edges and refrigerate for about 30–60 minutes, until firm.

Preheat the oven to 400°F. Prick the pastry all over, line with parchment paper and fill with baking weights. Bake in the preheated oven for 15 minutes, then remove the paper and weights and bake for 10–15 minutes more, until just golden. Let the tart shell cool slightly before filling. Leave the oven on.

To make the filling, put the eggs, crème fraîche, and a large pinch of salt in a bowl and whisk well. Slice each goat cheese into 3 rounds and arrange in the tart shell. Pour in the egg mixture and sprinkle with the Gruyère. Sprinkle the chives over the top.

Bake in the still hot oven for 20–30 minutes, until browned. Serve warm with a leafy salad greens.

Soups

Soupe au pistou

This recipe is a staple of Provençal cuisine. Purists will tell you that aged Gouda is imperative. The reason, according to one story, is that this soup was invented by Italian workers building the railway in the hills above Nice, who used the Dutch cheese because there was a lot of it in transit at the port.

3 tablespoons olive oil

1 onion, chopped

1 small fennel bulb, quartered, cored, and chopped

2 zucchini, chopped

8 oz. new potatoes, chopped

2 tomatoes, skinned, seeded, and chopped

2 quarts vegetable or chicken stock

a sprig of thyme

2 cups canned cannellini beans, drained

2 cups canned kidney beans, drained

6 oz. green beans, cut into 1-inch pieces

2 oz. spaghetti, broken into pieces

1⅓ cups finely grated cheese (aged Gouda or Parmesan)

coarse sea salt and freshly ground black pepper

Pistou

6 garlic cloves

leaves from a small bunch of basil

6 tablespoons extra virgin olive oil

Serves 4—6

Heat the oil in a large saucepan or casserole dish. Add the onion, fennel, and zucchini and cook over medium heat for about 10 minutes, until browned. Add the potatoes, tomatoes, stock, and thyme. Bring to a boil, then cover and simmer gently for 15 minutes.

Add the cannellini and kidney beans and simmer, covered, for 15 minutes more. Taste and adjust the seasoning. Add the green beans and the spaghetti and cook for about 10 minutes more, until the pasta is tender. Cover and let stand. Ideally, the soup should rest for at least a few hours before serving, or make one day in advance and refrigerate. (Do not make the pistou until you are ready to serve; it is best fresh, and the basil and garlic should not be cooked.)

To make the pistou, put the garlic, basil, and oil in a small food processor and blend until well chopped. You can also make it using a mortar and pestle, starting with the garlic and finishing with the oil, added gradually. It is more authentic, but I've never been very good at this method.

To serve, heat the soup and pass round the pistou and cheese, to be stirred in to taste. The soup can also be served at room temperature.

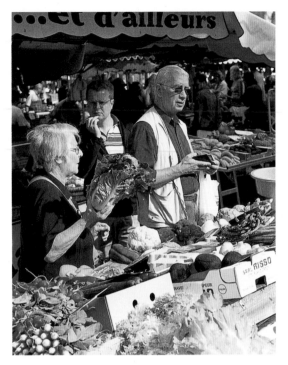

A classic case of less is more. This soup is soothing and restorative, and deliciously delicate, despite its rustic origins. Home-made salt pork makes all the difference to the taste and is very simple to make. If you don't have time to salt the pork yourself, buy a smoked pork knuckle from the butcher and proceed as in the main recipe. Your butcher should also be able to supply the pickling salt.

Cabbage soup Soupe au chou

1½ lbs. pork belly

4 oz. pickling salt

1 onion, studded with a clove

1 fresh bay leaf

1 cabbage

1 inner celery rib with leaves,
  cut into chunks

7 carrots, cut into chunks

4 turnips, cut into chunks

1 tablespoon unsalted butter,
  plus more for serving

1¾ lbs. small new potatoes, peeled

coarse sea salt

Serves 4—6

Three days before you plan to serve the soup, put the pork belly slices in a shallow non-reactive dish and add water to cover. Add the salt and stir until dissolved. Cover and refrigerate for 3 days, turning occasionally.

The day of serving, remove the pork belly from its brine and rinse. Put the pork and onion in a large saucepan with 3 quarts water. Bring to a boil and skim off any foam that rises to the surface, then reduce the heat, cover, and let simmer.

Meanwhile, bring another saucepan of water to the boil with a bay leaf. When it boils, add the cabbage and blanch for 5 minutes. Remove the cabbage and drain. When cool enough to handle, slice the cabbage.

Add the sliced cabbage, celery, carrots, turnips, and butter to the pork. Taste for seasoning; it may not need any salt because of the salt pork. Return to a boil, then lower the heat, cover, and simmer for about 30 minutes.

Add the potatoes and cook for 20–25 minutes, until tender. To serve, remove the pork belly and cut into bite-size pieces. Trim off any rind and discard any bones. Return the pork pieces to the soup and serve hot, with a spoonful of butter in each bowl and thick slices of country bread.

Kitchen garden soup · Soupe du potager

An old-fashioned nourishing soup, full of healthy green things. If you do not have sorrel growing in your garden (or available in your supermarket), it can be omitted.

1 fresh bay leaf

1 small cabbage, quartered

4 tablespoons unsalted butter

2 leeks, halved and sliced

1 onion, chopped

2 teaspoons fine sea salt

8 oz. new potatoes, chopped

a handful of flat-leaf parsley, chopped

2 cups fresh shelled peas

1 romaine lettuce heart, quartered and sliced thinly

a bunch of sorrel, sliced

unsalted butter and/or crème fraîche, to serve (optional)

sea salt and freshly ground black pepper

Serves 4—6

Put the bay leaf in a large saucepan of water and bring to a boil. Add the cabbage quarters and blanch for 3 minutes. Drain the cabbage, pat dry and slice it thinly.

Heat the butter in a large saucepan. Add the cabbage, leeks, onion, and 2 teaspoons salt and cook for 5–10 minutes, until softened. Add the potatoes, parsley, and 2 quarts water. Add more salt and pepper to taste and simmer gently for 40 minutes.

Stir in the peas, lettuce, and sorrel and cook for 10 minutes more. Taste for seasoning. Ladle into bowls, add 1 tablespoon of butter and/or crème fraîche, if using, to each and serve.

Vegetable bouillabaisse Bouillabaisse borgne

It is difficult to make true bouillabaisse outside France because so many of the fish used are found only in the Mediterranean. But here's a very good vegetable-only alternative, with all the same flavors, including the best part—the chile-spiked rouille sauce. Traditional versions include a poached egg, which I have omitted.

4 tablespoons olive oil

2 leeks, white part only, halved lengthwise, then sliced crosswise

1 large onion, coarsely chopped

1 fennel bulb, halved, cored, and chopped

3 garlic cloves, crushed

3 large ripe tomatoes, skinned, seeded, and chopped

5 medium new potatoes, cubed

2 quarts vegetable stock or water*

1 fresh bay leaf

a sprig of thyme

a strip of peel from 1 unwaxed orange

1 teaspoon good-quality saffron threads

1 baguette loaf, sliced, for croûtons

1½ cups freshly grated Gruyère cheese

coarse sea salt and freshly ground black pepper

a handful of chopped flat-leaf parsley, to serve

Rouille

3 garlic cloves, very finely chopped

1–2 red chiles, seeded, and very finely chopped

1 egg yolk, at room temperature

about 1¼ cups extra virgin olive oil

sea salt and freshly ground black pepper

Serves 4–6

Heat the oil in a large saucepan. Add the leeks, onions, and fennel and cook for about 10 minutes, until just beginning to brown. Stir in the garlic, tomatoes, potatoes, and 1 teaspoon salt and cook for 1 minute. Add the stock, bay leaf, thyme, orange peel, and saffron and stir. Bring to a boil, reduce the heat, and simmer gently for about 40 minutes, until the potatoes are tender. Add salt and pepper to taste, cover, and let stand for at least 1 hour, or let cool and refrigerate overnight.

Before you serve, make the croûtons. Preheat the oven to 350°F. Arrange the baguette slices in a single layer on a baking sheet. Bake in the preheated oven for about 5–8 minutes, until golden. Set aside.

To make the rouille, put the garlic, chiles, and egg yolk in a small, deep bowl. Beat well. Add the oil a little at a time and beating vigorously, until the mixture is thick like mayonnaise. Season to taste with salt and pepper.

To serve, warm the soup if necessary. Put 2–3 croûtons in each soup plate, sprinkle with the grated cheese and ladle in the soup. Sprinkle with chopped parsley and serve with the rouille, to be stirred in according to taste.

French onion soup

Soupe gratinée à l'oignon

Although this soup is synonymous with bistro eating, it is also associated with another tradition. At French weddings, especially in the countryside, it was often served in the early hours of the morning, as a restorative after a long night of celebrating. This recipe is a simplified version, the sort of thing that's ideal when it's chilly outside, people are hungry inside and there's not much more than a few onions lurking about.

3 tablespoons unsalted butter

1 tablespoon olive oil

3 large onions, about 3 lbs., thinly sliced

2 garlic cloves, crushed

1 tablespoon all-purpose flour

1 quart beef, chicken, or vegetable stock

2¼ cups dry white wine

1 fresh bay leaf

2 sprigs of thyme

1 baguette, sliced

1½ cups freshly grated Gruyère cheese (about 5 oz.)

coarse sea salt and freshly ground black pepper

Serves 4—6

Put the butter and oil in a large saucepan and melt over medium heat. Add the onions and cook over low heat for 15–20 minutes, until soft.

Add the garlic and flour and cook, stirring for about 1 minute. Add the stock, wine, bay leaf, and thyme. Season with salt and pepper and bring to a boil. Boil for 1 minute, then lower the heat and simmer very gently for 20 minutes. Taste and adjust the seasoning. At this point, the soup will be cooked, but standing time will improve the flavor—at least 30 minutes.

Before serving, preheat the broiler. Put the baguette slices on a baking sheet and brown under the broiler until lightly toasted. Set aside. Do not turn the broiler off.

To serve, ladle the soup into ovenproof bowls and top with a few toasted baguette rounds. Sprinkle grated cheese over the top and cook under the still hot broiler until browned and bubbling. Serve immediately.

Basque fish soup Ttoro

France has many fish soups but only this one includes hot chiles. Another plus is that it can be made successfully without hard-to-come-by Mediterranean fish and, if you use good-quality fresh fish stock, it's very quick to make. The bones and shrimp shells add flavor, as well as making it a bit messy, but this is fishermen's fare, so roll up your sleeves and enjoy.

2 tablespoons olive oil

1 red bell pepper, halved, seeded, and sliced

1 onion, halved and sliced

3 garlic cloves, crushed

1 green chile, seeded and chopped

¼ teaspoon hot paprika

a sprig of thyme

1 cup canned chopped tomatoes

1½ quarts fresh fish stock

8 oz. monkfish fillet, cut into bite-size pieces

1 lb. hake or cod steaks

8 oz. unpeeled shrimp tails

1 cup dry white wine

1 lb. fresh mussels*

a handful of flat-leaf parsley, chopped

Garlic croûtons

1 baguette, sliced

2 garlic cloves, peeled

Serves 4—6

Heat the oil in a stockpot or large saucepan. Add the bell pepper and onion and cook for about 5 minutes, until browned. Stir in the garlic, chile, paprika, thyme, and tomatoes and cook for 5 minutes more.

Add the stock, monkfish, hake, and shrimp. Bring to a boil, skim off the foam and simmer gently for 10–15 minutes, until the fish is cooked through.

Meanwhile, make the garlic croûtons. Preheat the oven to 350°F. Arrange the baguette slices in a single layer on a baking sheet. Bake in the preheated oven for 5–8 minutes, until golden. Let cool slightly, then rub with garlic cloves and set aside.

Pour the wine into a large saucepan with a lid and bring to a boil for 1 minute, then remove from the heat. Add the prepared mussels to the wine, cover, and steam over high heat for 2–3 minutes, just until opened. Remove the mussels from their shells, discarding any that do not open.

Add the mussels and cooking liquid to the soup and stir well. Sprinkle with parsley and serve immediately, with the garlic croûtons.

*NOTE To prepare mussels, start 15 minutes before you are ready to use. Rinse them in cold water and tap any open ones against the work surface. If they don't close, discard them. Scrub the others with a stiff brush and scrape off any barnacles. Pull off and discard the wiry beards.

Meat

Pork in cider with potatoes and apples

Porc au cidre aux deux pommes

If it has apples and cream, then it must be from Normandy. The cider is a good clue as well, and it provides a luxuriously rich sauce for the long-simmered pork. Unlike recipes from more southerly realms, this is subtle and delicate, but no less powerful for its discretion. A good dish for all the family, as children (and adults) enjoy sweet things to accompany their meat. Serve with the cider used in cooking, or a red wine from the Loire.

2 tablespoons unsalted butter

2 onions, sliced

1 tablespoon safflower oil

1 pork middle leg roast, about 3½ lbs., fat trimmed

1½ quarts hard dry cider

2 sprigs of thyme

1¼ lbs. new potatoes, peeled, and halved lengthwise

½ cup heavy cream

coarse sea salt and freshly ground black pepper

Apples

4 tablespoons unsalted butter

5 tart apples, such as Braeburn or Cox's, peeled, cored and sliced

a large flameproof casserole dish

Serves 4

Preheat the oven to 300°F.

Melt the butter in a large flameproof casserole dish. Add the onions and cook gently for about 5 minutes, until softened but not browned. Remove the onions. Add the oil, increase the heat, add the pork and cook until browned all over. Remove and season well with salt and pepper.

Add some of the cider to the casserole dish, heat and scrape the bottom of the pan. Return the meat, onions, remaining cider, and thyme. Season lightly and bring to a boil. Boil for 1 minute, skim off any foam that rises to the surface, then reduce the heat, cover, and cook in the preheated oven for 4 hours. Turn the pork regularly and taste and adjust the seasoning half-way through the cooking time.

One hour before the end of the cooking time, add the potatoes and continue cooking.

Remove from the oven, transfer the pork and potatoes to a plate and cover with foil to keep it warm. Cook the sauce over high heat for 10–15 minutes to reduce slightly. Taste and adjust the seasoning.

Meanwhile, to cook the apples, melt the butter in a large sauté pan, add the apples and cook over high heat for 5–10 minutes, until browned and tender. Do not crowd the pan; use 2 pans if necessary.

To serve, slice the pork and arrange on plates with the potatoes and apples. Stir the cream into the sauce and serve immediately.

Pork chops with piquant sauce Côtes de porc charcutière

This is the sort of basic fare you'll find in cafés and bistros all over France. The mustardy-vinegary sauce is ideal with pork. Cornichons are the best part so be sure to use the real thing. They must be small and, ideally, bottled in France. I've seen other tiny gherkins labelled as cornichons but, unless they come from France, they never taste as I expect. Serve with mashed potatoes.

4 thick-cut pork chops, rind removed

extra virgin olive oil

coarse sea salt and freshly ground black pepper

Piquant sauce

¼ cup wine, dry white or red

1 cup fresh chicken stock

¼ cup tarragon or sherry vinegar

4 tablespoons unsalted butter

3 shallots, finely chopped

1 tablespoon all-purpose flour

2 teaspoons tomato paste

1 teaspoon coarse Dijon mustard

8 French cornichons, sliced into rounds

a sprig of tarragon, leaves stripped and chopped

a small handful of flat-leaf parsley, chopped

a ridged stovetop grill pan

Serves 2—4

To make the sauce, put the wine and stock in a small saucepan. Bring to a boil for 1 minute, then stir in the vinegar. Set aside.

Melt the butter in another saucepan. Add the shallots and cook for 3–5 minutes, until soft. Add the flour and cook, stirring for 1 minute. Add the warm stock mixture and tomato paste and mix well. Simmer gently for 15 minutes.

Meanwhile, to cook the pork chops, rub a ridged stovetop grill pan with the oil and heat on high. When hot, add the pork chops and cook for 4–5 minutes. Turn and cook the other side for 3–4 minutes. Remove from the heat and season on both sides with salt and pepper.

Stir the mustard, cornichons, tarragon, and parsley into the sauce and serve immediately, with the pork chops and plenty of mashed potatoes.

If you thought pork was bland, think again. It is actually a spectacular vehicle for all sorts of flavors, and responds remarkably well to marinating. The French have known this for years, because the idea for this recipe came from one of my favorite cookbooks, *La Cuisine de Mme Saint-Ange*, first published in 1927. Any cut of pork can be marinated, from a few hours to overnight, and the leftovers are as good, if not better, than the original. Serve with something creamy, like Cauliflower Gratin (page 115), or roasted vegetables.

Marinated pork roast Côti de porc mariné

1 boneless pork loin roast,
  about 3 lbs.

1 large onion, sliced

2 carrots, sliced

1 celery rib, with leaves

Marinade

750-ml bottle dry white wine

3 tablespoons white wine vinegar

2 garlic cloves, peeled and sliced

1 fresh bay leaf

2–3 fresh sage leaves

a sprig of thyme

2 tablespoons coarse sea salt

1 tablespoon sugar

1 teaspoon black peppercorns

a large roasting pan

Serves 4—6

Two days before serving, mix all the ingredients for the marinade together in a large non-reactive bowl. Add the pork and vegetables, cover, and refrigerate for 2 days, turning the pork regularly.

When ready to cook, preheat the oven to 400°F. Remove the pork from the marinade and put it in a large roasting pan. Add the vegetables and flavorings from the marinade.

Cook in the preheated oven for 1½ hours, basting occasionally with the marinating liquid. Serve in slices with the side dish of your choice.

Cassoulet

A classic from the south-west, adapted for those of us outside France. Do not let the long list put you off. This is actually quite easy: cook the beans, cook the meat stew, brown the duck and sausages, then put it all together. That's it. You do need good sausages, with as high a pork content as possible. Duck confit is sold canned in large supermarkets, or in good gourmet stores. You will also need several large pots, a large dish to cook it in, and very hungry friends.

Beans

1¾ lbs. dried haricot beans

10 oz. thick-sliced country ham

a piece of salt pork

1 carrot, chopped

1 fresh bay leaf

1 onion, studded with 2 cloves

4 whole garlic cloves

1 teaspoon salt

Meat

1 tablespoon olive oil

1½ lbs. pork spareribs

1½ lbs. boneless lamb shoulder, cubed

1 onion, chopped

3 garlic cloves, crushed

2 cups canned chopped tomatoes

1 fresh bay leaf

2 quarts fresh chicken stock

6 canned duck confit thigh pieces

10 Toulouse sausages
    or other pure pork sausages

1 cup fresh bread crumbs

coarse sea salt and freshly
    ground black pepper

a large casserole dish

Serves 8

In the morning, one day before serving, put the beans in a bowl with plenty of cold water and let soak (soak for at least 6 hours, or start 2 days early and soak overnight.)

Drain the beans. Put in a large saucepan with cold water to cover, bring to a boil, and simmer for 10 minutes. Drain. Return the beans to the pan and add the ham, salt pork, carrot, bay leaf, onion, and garlic. Cover with water by about 2 inches and bring to a boil. Lower the heat and simmer gently for 1 hour. Add 1 teaspoon salt and continue cooking for 30 minutes more. Let cool, then refrigerate overnight; do not drain.

Meanwhile, to prepare the meat stew, heat the oil in a large sauté pan. Add the spareribs and lamb and fry until brown. Add the onion and garlic and cook for about 3 minutes, until just soft. Add the tomatoes, bay leaf, and stock. Season. Bring to a boil, skim off the foam, then lower the heat, cover and simmer gently for 1½ hours. Add salt and pepper to taste. Let cool, cover, and refrigerate overnight.

The next day, about 3 hours before serving, discard the fat from the top of the stew. Remove the meat from the spareribs, return to the stew, and discard the bones. Bring the beans to room temperature (or warm slightly), drain and reserve the liquid. Season to taste.

Heat a large sauté pan, add the duck confit pieces, and fry until browned. Remove, cut the thighs into pieces and set aside. In the same pan, brown the sausages. Do not discard the cooking fat.

Preheat the oven to 425°F. Now you are ready to assemble. Remove the salt pork and ham from the beans and put in a large casserole dish. Top with one-third of the beans. Arrange the duck confit in the middle (so that you know where to find it when serving), and the sausages all around the edge. Spread the meat stew on top. Cover with the remaining beans. Spoon in some of the reserved bean liquid (you should just be able to see it), then sprinkle with a thin layer of bread crumbs. Pour in the duck and sausage fat. Cook in the preheated oven for 30 minutes.

Reduce the oven temperature to 375°F. Gently break up the crust on top, then spoon over some more bean liquid and sprinkle with more bread crumbs. Continue checking, about every 30 minutes or so, adding more liquid as necessary; be sure not to let the cassoulet dry out. When the cassoulet has cooked for 2 hours and the crust is well browned, remove from the oven.

Serve hot, allowing a portion of confit, the sausages, and plenty of beans for each person.

Steak and fries

Steak frites

Nothing says bistro better than this. The shallot butter is a fancy flourish; it is just as authentic to serve as is, with nothing more than Dijon mustard, for both the steak and the fries (but no ketchup, please!) The secret of cooking great fries is to use a good floury variety of potato and to cook them twice. They should be dry, rustling, crisp and well seasoned.

4 sirloin or rib eye steaks, about 10 oz. each, 1 inch thick

1 tablespoon safflower oil

coarse sea salt and freshly ground black pepper

Shallot butter

1 stick unsalted butter, softened

2 shallots, finely chopped

⅔ cup red wine

a large sprig of tarragon

several sprigs of flat-leaf parsley

1 teaspoon coarse sea salt

½ teaspoon freshly ground black pepper

Fries

1 lb. floury potatoes

safflower oil, for deep frying

sea salt, to serve

a large saucepan with frying basket

a ridged stovetop grill pan

Serves 4

To make the shallot butter, put about 2 tablespoons of the butter in a saucepan and melt over low heat. Add the shallots and cook until softened. Add the wine, bring to a boil, and cook until syrupy and the wine has almost completely evaporated. Set aside to cool.

Put the cooled shallots, remaining butter, tarragon, parsley, salt, and pepper in a small food processor and blend briefly. Transfer the mixture to a piece of parchment paper and shape into a log. Roll up and chill until firm.

To prepare the fries, peel the potatoes and cut into ¼-inch slices. Cut the slices into ¼-inch strips. Put into a bowl of ice water for at least 5 minutes. When ready to cook, drain and pat dry with paper towels.

Fill a large saucepan one-third full with oil. Heat the oil to 375°F or until a cube of bread browns in 30 seconds. Working in batches, put 2 large handfuls of potato strips into the frying basket, lower carefully into the oil, and fry for about 4 minutes. Remove and drain on paper towels. Repeat until all the strips have been cooked. Skim any debris off the top of the oil, reheat to the same temperature, then fry the strips for a second time (about 2 minutes), until crisp and golden. Remove and drain on paper towels, then sprinkle with salt. Keep hot in the oven until ready to serve

To prepare the steaks, rub them on both sides with the oil. Heat a ridged stovetop grill pan until hot. Cook the steaks for just 1½–2 minutes. Turn and cook the other side for 1–2 minutes. This will produce a rare steak. To produce a medium-rare steak, turn and cook again on both sides for 2–3 minutes more. Remove from the pan and season both sides. Let stand for a few minutes. Serve with rounds of the shallot butter and the hot fries.

Braised steak with anchovies and capers

Brouffade

The sailors who used to guide barges up and down the Rhône, from Arles to Lyon, were lucky men indeed. They invented this dish and, I assume, ate it often. If I were having my last supper, this would be it, with mashed potatoes, a green salad, and a good red Rhône wine.

4 thick rump steaks, about
    10 oz. each

4 onions, halved and sliced

3 tablespoons capers, drained

12 French cornichons, chopped

10 anchovy fillets packed in oil,
    finely chopped

1 tablespoon all-purpose flour

3 tablespoons red wine vinegar

Marinade

⅔ cup olive oil

8 garlic cloves, crushed

a small handful of flat-leaf parsley,
    chopped

1 teaspoon coarsely ground
    black pepper

1 fresh bay leaf

a sprig of thyme

1 inner celery rib, with leaves

a large casserole dish

Serves 4—6

One day before serving, mix all of the marinade ingredients together in a shallow non-reactive dish. Add the steaks and turn to coat well with the mixture. Cover with plastic wrap and refrigerate overnight, turning at least twice.

Preheat the oven to 300°F.

Put the onions, capers, and cornichons in a bowl and toss well. Put the anchovies and flour in a small bowl and blend well. Remove the meat from the marinade and set aside. Stir the anchovies and vinegar into the marinade.

Put one-third of the onion mixture in the casserole dish and put 2 steaks on top, side by side. Spoon in half of the marinade, spreading it over the meat. Top with half the remaining onion mixture, then the remaining steaks. Spoon over the rest of the marinade and top with the rest of the onion mixture.

Pour in about 1 cup water. Cut a piece of parchment paper to about the diameter of the casserole dish and put this on top of the onions to help seal in all the juices. Cover with the lid and cook in the preheated oven for 3 hours. Serve immediately with mashed potatoes and salad greens.

Braised beef brisket with carrots

Boeuf aux carottes

This humble French culinary masterpiece rates high on the scale of life's little pleasures. It has no precise geographical origin—everyone makes it, and rightly so. The beef practically melts in your mouth and the broth is rich, sweet, and buttery from all the carrots. A prime candidate for potatoes, tagliatelle or, even better, the Macaroni Gratin (page 91). French Beans with Garlic (page 110) would also be delicious. Experiment with different cuts of beef—anything that will stand up to long, slow simmering.

2 tablespoons olive oil

3 lbs. brisket, rolled and tied by the butcher

3 lbs. carrots

6 oz. bacon lardons

1 onion, halved and sliced

2 garlic cloves, crushed

1 fresh bay leaf

a sprig of thyme

1 small leafy celery rib

2 cups dry white wine

coarse sea salt and freshly ground black pepper

a large flameproof casserole dish

Serves 4—6

Preheat the oven to 300°F.

Heat 1 tablespoon of the oil in a large flameproof casserole dish. Add the meat and cook until browned on all sides. Transfer to a plate and sprinkle generously with salt.

Heat the remaining oil in the casserole dish, add the carrots and 1 teaspoon salt and cook for 3–5 minutes, stirring occasionally, until brown. Remove and set aside.

Put the lardons and onion in the casserole dish and cook over high heat for 3–5 minutes, until browned.

Add the garlic, bay leaf, thyme, celery, carrots, and beef. Pour in the wine and add water almost to cover. Bring to a boil, skim, then cover with a lid and cook in the preheated oven for 3 hours. Turn the meat over at least once during cooking.

Sprinkle with pepper and serve with your choice of accompaniments.

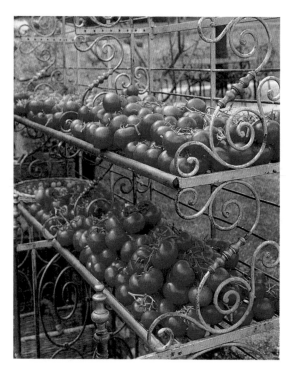

Stuffed tomatoes

Tomates farcies

This classic dish is a reminder that good French food is not about expensive cuts, or elaborate sauces. In fact, the real recipe calls for leftover beef from a stew—home economy at its best. If you have any leftovers from the Braised Beef Brisket (page 48), then use them. It's also nice if you mix leftovers, like lamb and pork, with the beef. This summery dish is ideal for lunch or a light dinner, served with salad greens and a light-medium red wine.

2 tablespoons olive oil

4 shallots, finely chopped

3 large garlic cloves, crushed

4 oz. bacon lardons

3 tablespoons dry white wine

12 large tomatoes

13 oz. ground beef

1 egg

4 tablespoons fresh bread crumbs

½ teaspoon dried herbes
de provence

a handful of flat-leaf parsley,
finely chopped

coarse sea salt and freshly
ground black pepper

*a baking dish, greased with
2 tablespoons olive oil*

Serves 4—6

Preheat the oven to 400°F.

Heat the oil in a large sauté pan. Add the shallots and garlic and cook for 3–5 minutes, until softened but not browned. Add the bacon lardons and fry for 3–5 minutes, until just beginning to brown. Stir in the wine and cook until it has evaporated. Transfer to a large bowl and let cool.

Slice the tops off of the tomatoes and set the tops aside. Carefully deseed with a spoon. Pat the insides dry with paper towels and season with salt and pepper. Set aside.

Add the beef to the shallot mixture, then stir in the egg, bread crumbs, herbs, parsley, and 1 teaspoon salt. Cook a small piece of the stuffing mixture in a sauté pan, taste for seasoning, adding more salt if necessary.

Fill the tomato shells with the beef mixture, mounding it at the top. Replace the tomato tops and arrange apart in the prepared baking dish. Cook in the preheated oven for about 30 minutes, until cooked through and browned.

*VARIATION Another speciality from Provence, les petits farcis (little stuffed vegetables), can be made using the same stuffing to fill a variety of vegetables: zucchini, eggplants, and bell peppers are ideal, but you can also use artichokes and mushrooms. Provençal dishes often have a bread crumb topping, so add a handful of chopped fresh parsley, crushed garlic, and some grated Parmesan to fresh bread crumbs and sprinkle over the tops before baking.

meat 51

Beef and potato gratin Hachis parmentier

Antoine-Augustin Parmentier introduced potatoes to the French public in the late 18th century, and this dish of ground beef nestled between two layers of creamy mashed potatoes is a tribute to him. Not as glamorous as a bridge over the Seine perhaps, but delicious nonetheless. The traditional recipe calls for leftover cooked beef, specifically stewed or boiled beef, so use that if you have some. The taste benefits from flavorful leftovers, but mince that has been well seasoned and cooked in a bit of wine comes a close second. Serve with peas or haricots verts and a fruity red wine.

3 tablespoons unsalted butter or
   2 tablespoons safflower oil

2 onions, chopped

2 garlic cloves

1½ lbs. ground beef

3 oz. bacon, finely chopped

½ cup dry white wine

a handful of flat-leaf parsley,
   chopped

a sprig of thyme, leaves stripped

2 tablespoons tomato paste

¼ cup freshly grated Gruyère
   cheese (about 2 oz.)

coarse sea salt and freshly ground
   black pepper

Potato purée

4 lbs. potatoes

1 fresh bay leaf

1 cup hot milk

1 stick unsalted butter, cut
   into pieces

sea salt

*a baking dish, about 12 inches
   long, greased with butter*

Serves 4—6

To prepare the purée, put the potatoes and bay leaf in a saucepan of cold water. Bring to a boil, add salt, and cook until tender. Drain.

Put the potatoes in a large bowl and mash coarsely with a wooden spoon. Using an electric mixer, gradually add the milk and butter, beating until the mixture is smooth. Add salt and whisk well. If the potatoes are very dry, add more milk. Taste, then add more butter and/or salt as necessary and set aside.

Heat the butter in a sauté pan, add the onions and cook over high heat for 3–5 minutes, until just brown. Add the garlic, beef, and chopped bacon and cook until almost completely browned. Add the wine and cook until it has almost evaporated. Stir in the parsley, thyme leaves, and tomato paste. Taste and adjust the seasoning with salt and pepper.

Preheat the oven to 400°F.

Spread half the potatoes in the prepared baking dish. Add the beef mixture and level with a spoon. Spread with the remaining potatoes. Sprinkle with the cheese and bake in the preheated oven for about 25–30 minutes, until golden. Serve with the accompaniment of your choice.

Spring lamb stew with vegetables Navarin d'agneau

This reminds me of long Sunday family lunches, the ones that go on almost until dinner, the likes of which I'd never known before living in France. To re-create something similar, start with apéritifs and nibbles at midday, then serve this with boiled baby new potatoes and a bottle of St-Emilion. Follow with a green salad and a generous cheese platter. A slice of the Simple Apple Tart (see page 142) before coffee makes the perfect ending.

1 tablespoon safflower oil

1½ lbs. boneless rib lamb chops, cubed

1 lb. boneless loin lamb chops, each one cut into several pieces

1 tablespoon all-purpose flour

2 ripe tomatoes, skinned, seeded, and chopped

2 garlic cloves, crushed

2¼ cups lamb or chicken stock

1 fresh bay leaf

a sprig of thyme

4 baby carrots, cut into 1 inch pieces

8 oz. baby leeks, cut into 2-inch lengths

8 oz. baby turnips

8 oz. sugar snap peas

a handful of flat-leaf parsley, chopped

coarse sea salt and freshly ground black pepper

a large flameproof casserole dish

Serves 4

Heat the oil in a large flameproof casserole dish. Add the lamb and brown the pieces on all sides, in batches if necessary. When all the lamb has been browned, return it all to the casserole dish, lower the heat slightly and stir in a pinch of salt and the flour. Cook, stirring to coat evenly, for 1 minute.

Add the tomatoes and garlic. Stir in the stock, bay leaf, and thyme. Bring to a boil and skim off any foam that rises to the surface. Reduce the heat, then cover and simmer gently for 40 minutes.

Add the carrots, leeks, and turnips and cook for 25 minutes more. Taste and adjust the seasoning with salt and pepper.

Add the sugar snap peas and cook for about 7 minutes, until tender. Sprinkle with the parsley and serve immediately.

Leg of lamb with anchovies Agneau à la gasconnade

Gasconnade refers to the anchovies and it is a traditional way of flavoring lamb in the south-west of France. The slow cooking in wine mellows the anchovies, making for a rich sauce and very tender meat. Serve with tagliatelle, potatoes, or flageolet beans.

1 leg of lamb (3 lbs), trimmed

14 anchovy fillets

2 tablespoons olive oil

2 onions, chopped

2 carrots, chopped

3 garlic cloves, crushed

2 tomatoes, skinned, seeded, and chopped

750-ml bottle red wine

2 sprigs of thyme

1 fresh bay leaf

1 tablespoon tomato paste

coarse sea salt

a large flameproof casserole dish

Serves 4—6

Preheat the oven to 350°F.

Make slits all over the lamb and insert the anchovy fillets, as you do when studding with garlic.

Heat the oil in a large flameproof casserole dish. Add the lamb and brown on all sides. Remove, season lightly, and set aside.

Put the onions and carrots in the casserole dish and cook over high heat for 3–5 minutes, until lightly browned. Add the garlic and chopped tomatoes and cook for 1 minute. Add the wine, thyme, bay leaf, and tomato paste and bring to a boil. Boil for 1 minute, then add the lamb.

Cover with the lid, transfer to the preheated oven, and cook for 1½ hours, turning every 20 minutes or so. Remove the thyme and bay leaf and serve with the accompaniment of your choice.

Poultry and game

This poor man's version of a dish in which truffle slices are stuffed under the chicken skin makes a nice change from ordinary roast chicken. The perfume of bay leaves and thyme delicately flavors the chicken flesh, while the tartness of the lemon keeps it lively.

Roast chicken with herbs and lemon

Poulet rôti aux herbes et citron

1 free-range chicken, about 3 lbs.
2 lemons, 1 quartered, 1 sliced
6 large fresh bay leaves
2 sprigs of thyme
1–2 tablespoons olive oil
1 teaspoon dried thyme
1 onion, sliced in rounds
1 cup dry white wine or water
1 tablespoon unsalted butter
coarse sea salt

a large roasting pan with a rack

Serves 4

Preheat the oven to 425°F.

Season the inside of the chicken generously and stuff with the lemon quarters, 2 of the bay leaves, and the thyme sprigs. Using your fingers, separate the skin from the breast meat to create a pocket and put 1 bay leaf on each side of the breast, underneath the skin. Put the remaining bay leaves under the skin of the thighs. Rub the outside of the chicken all over with the oil, season generously, and sprinkle over the dried thyme.

Put the chicken on its side on a rack set over a roasting pan. Add water to fill the bottom of the pan by about ½ inch and add the sliced lemon and onion. Cook in the preheated oven for 40 minutes, then turn the chicken on its other side. Continue roasting the chicken for about 40 minutes more, until cooked through and the juices run clear when a thigh is pierced with a skewer. Add extra water to the roasting pan if necessary during cooking.

Transfer the chicken to a plate, cover, and let stand for 10 minutes. Add the wine to the pan juices and cook over high heat for 3–5 minutes, scraping the bottom of the pan. Stir in the butter. Carve and serve with the pan juices.

Chicken with bell peppers, onions, ham, and tomatoes   Poulet basquaise

Like all traditional dishes, there are many versions of this recipe; some call only for green bell peppers, some use only onions and chiles. I think chiles are imperative, and if you want to be completely authentic, use piment d'Espelette, which is a most delicious little chile grown in the Basque region of France, but very difficult to find outside this area. They are pleasantly spicy without being overpowering, so whatever chile you use, resist the temptation to overdo it. Serve with rice.

2 tablespoons olive oil

1 free-range chicken, about 4 lbs., cut into 8 pieces

2 onions, sliced

2 red bell peppers, halved, seeded, and sliced

2 yellow bell peppers, halved, seeded, and sliced

2–4 large garlic cloves, crushed

2 small hot green chiles, seeded and thinly sliced (or ½ teaspoon dried hot pepper flakes)

1 thick slice jambon de Bayonne or other unsmoked ham, about 1 inch thick and 6 oz., cut into strips

2 lbs. ripe tomatoes, skinned, seeded, and chopped

coarse sea salt and freshly ground black pepper

Serves 4

Heat the oil in a large sauté pan with a lid, add the chicken pieces skin-side down and cook for 5–10 minutes, until brown. Don't crowd the pan; if you can't fit all the pieces at once, brown in batches. Transfer the chicken to a plate, season well with salt, and set aside.

Add the onions and bell peppers to the pan, season with salt and black pepper, then cook over medium heat for 15–20 minutes, until soft. Stir in the garlic, chiles, and ham and cook for 1 minute. Add the tomatoes, mix well, then add all the chicken pieces and bury them under the sauce.

Cover and cook over low heat for 30–40 minutes, until the chicken is tender. Serve with rice.

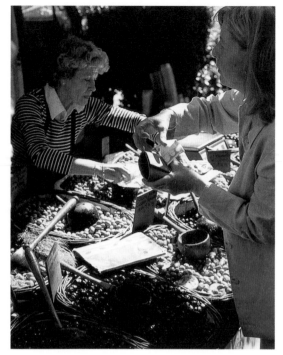

Chicken with tomato, garlic, and olives

Poulet sauté niçoise

2 tablespoons olive oil

1 free-range chicken, about 4 lbs., cut into 6–8 pieces

8 garlic cloves, finely chopped

2 cups canned chopped tomatoes

a pinch of sugar

2 oz. black olives, preferably niçoise, pitted and coarsely chopped

coarse sea salt and freshly ground black pepper

leaves from a small bunch of fresh basil, torn

tagliatelle or rice, to serve

Serves 4—6

Poulet sauté is at home all over France, but I especially like this south-eastern version with its assertive flavors. It goes very well with fresh pasta such as tagliatelle or rice, and a sturdy red wine, such as a Collioure or Minervois.

Heat 1 tablespoon of the oil in a large sauté pan. Add the chicken pieces and brown on all sides. Transfer to a plate, salt generously, and set aside.

Add the remaining oil and garlic to the pan and cook for 1 minute; do not let the garlic burn. Add the tomatoes and sugar. Stir well and return the chicken pieces to the pan. Cover and simmer gently for 25–30 minutes, until the chicken is cooked.

Transfer the chicken pieces to a serving dish, then increase the heat and cook the sauce for about 10 minutes, to thicken it slightly. Season to taste, then stir in the olives. Pour the sauce over the chicken pieces, sprinkle with the basil, and serve immediately with tagliatelle or rice, as preferred.

A dish without a region, this is served pretty much all over France, in homes as well as restaurants. It's quick to make, if you get your butcher to cut up the chicken, and the flavor of tarragon lifts this out of the ordinary. Make this dish midweek and you'll have a lovely supper in under an hour, or serve it for your next dinner party and it will seem as if you slaved away all day. A red St-Estèphe or Ladoix would be the ideal wine.

Chicken with tarragon   Poulet sauté à l'estragon

1 tablespoon unsalted butter

1 tablespoon safflower oil

1 free-range corn-fed chicken, about 4 lbs., cut into 6–8 pieces

2 carrots, chopped

1 shallot, chopped

a sprig of thyme

2–3 sprigs of flat-leaf parsley

a bunch of tarragon

3 tablespoons crème fraîche or sour cream

coarse sea salt and freshly ground black pepper

Serves 4

Melt the butter and oil in a large sauté pan with a lid. Add the chicken pieces and cook for about 5 minutes, until brown. Put the browned chicken pieces on a plate and season well with salt and pepper.

Add the carrots and shallot to the pan and cook, stirring for 1–2 minutes. Return the chicken to the pan and add water to cover half-way. Add the thyme, parsley, and a few sprigs of tarragon. Cover and simmer gently for 30 minutes.

Meanwhile, strip the leaves from the remaining tarragon, chop them finely, and set aside. Add the stems to the cooking chicken.

Remove the chicken from the pan and put it in a serving dish. Remove and discard the tarragon stems.

Increase the heat and cook the sauce until it has reduced by half. Strain and return the sauce to the pan. Stir in the crème fraîche and the chopped tarragon. Heat briefly (do not let it reach a boil as the cream will split) and pour over the chicken. Serve immediately.

Guinea fowl with lentils — Pintade aux lentilles

If you can find a true guinea fowl, from a butcher or specialist supplier, then it will taste as it should. It is worth the effort to search out the real thing because supermarket guinea fowl is disappointing, to say the least. The flavor bears no resemblance to anything worth paying money for; you are better off buying an organic or free-range chicken, since the preparation is the same and the result will be superior. Fortunately, the lentils will never disappoint.

1 guinea fowl, about 3 lbs.

3 tablespoons olive oil

1 cup dried green lentils, preferably French

a sprig of thyme

1 fresh bay leaf

4 large shallots, chopped

2 carrots, chopped

5 oz. bacon lardons

1 cup white wine

coarse sea salt and freshly ground black pepper

a roasting pan with a rack

Serves 4

Preheat the oven to 425°F.

Rub the guinea fowl all over with 1 tablespoon of the olive oil and season well, inside and out. Put on a rack set in a roasting pan and cook in the preheated oven for about 1 hour, until browned and the juices run clear when the thigh is pierced with a skewer.

Meanwhile, put the lentils, thyme, and bay leaf into a saucepan and just cover with water. Bring to a boil, reduce the heat, cover with a lid, and simmer gently for about 25 minutes, until tender. Drain and season with salt.

Heat the remaining 2 tablespoons oil in a sauté pan. Add the shallots and carrots and cook for 3–5 minutes, until just tender. Stir in the bacon lardons and cook, stirring, until well browned. Add the wine and cook over high heat until reduced by half. Add the lentils, discard the herbs, and set aside.

Remove the guinea fowl from the oven, cover, and let stand for 10 minutes. Carve into serving pieces and serve immediately, with the lentils.

If you can find imported French duck magrets, they are worth buying, both for the flavor and for the size. If you use domestic duck breasts, cooking time will be less and you will probably need two per person. Serve with sautéed or roasted potatoes and a red wine such as Madiran.

Duck breasts with peppercorns

Magret de canard aux deux poivres

2 French duck magrets or 4 duck
  breasts, about 1½ lbs.

3 tablespoons Cognac

1 cup crème fraîche or sour cream

1 tablespoon green peppercorns
  in brine, drained

1 tablespoon coarsely ground
  black pepper

coarse sea salt

Serves 2

Trim the excess fat from around the duck breasts, then score the skin in a diamond pattern.

Heat a heavy sauté pan. When hot, add the duck skin-side first and cook for 7–8 minutes. Turn and cook the other side for 4–5 minutes, depending on thickness. Remove from the pan, season with salt, and keep warm.

Drain almost all the fat from the pan. Return to the heat and add the Cognac, scraping the bottom of the pan. Stir in the cream, green peppercorns, and black pepper. Cook for 1 minute.

Slice the duck diagonally lengthwise and put on serving plates. Pour the sauce over the top and serve immediately.

Rabbit with prunes

Lapin aux pruneaux

Rabbit and prunes don't really have a season, but this somehow seems right for fall, just the thing when the days are getting shorter and cooler, and it's nice to fill the house with appetizing aromas. A more apt name would be Drunken Rabbit, because there is so much wine, Cognac, and port. But prunes it is, and they do play a vital part, adding a pleasant sweetness to the rich, velvety sauce and salty bacon lardons. Serve it with fresh pasta tossed in butter—tagliatelle is ideal. Chicken can be substituted for the rabbit, but don't cook it for as long.

1 rabbit, cut into 7–8 pieces

2 tablespoons safflower oil

2 tablespoons unsalted butter

2 onions, halved and sliced

7 oz. bacon lardons

about 1 cup all-purpose flour

½ cup port

2½ cups plump prunes

1 tablespoon crème fraîche or
    sour cream

coarse sea salt and freshly ground
    black pepper

tagliatelle, to serve

Marinade

1 onion, chopped

1 carrot, chopped

2 garlic cloves, crushed

2 sprigs of thyme

1 fresh bay leaf

750-ml bottle red wine

1 cup Cognac

a few black or green peppercorns

a large flameproof casserole dish

Serves 4

One day before serving, mix all the marinade ingredients in a non-reactive bowl. Add the rabbit pieces, cover, and refrigerate overnight.

When ready to cook, remove the rabbit from the marinade, strain the liquid and reserve. Discard all the vegetables but keep the thyme and bay leaf. Pat the rabbit pieces dry with paper towels.

Heat 1 tablespoon of the oil and half the butter in a large flameproof casserole dish. Add the onions and bacon lardons and cook over high heat for 5 minutes, until brown. Remove from the casserole dish and set aside.

Put the flour on a plate and add the rabbit pieces, turning to coat lightly. Add the remaining oil and butter to the casserole dish and heat. When sizzling, put the rabbit pieces in the casserole dish and brown all over. Pour in the strained marinating liquid, bacon and onion mixture, and port. Add the reserved thyme and bay leaf and season with salt and pepper. Bring to a boil, skim off the foam, then lower the heat, cover, and simmer for 45 minutes. Season to taste.

Transfer the rabbit pieces to a plate, add the prunes, increase the heat and cook the sauce for 10–15 minutes more, until thickened. Stir in the crème fraîche, return the rabbit to the casserole dish and heat just to warm through; do not let it reach a boil. Serve with tagliatelle.

Fish and seafood

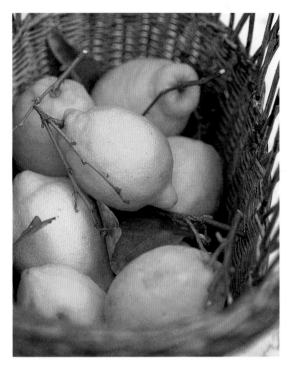

Sole meunière

I am utterly addicted to this dish with its buttery-lemony sauce. Sole is a well-crafted fish, both meaty and delicate at the same time, and is very easy to eat, bone-wise. Do not make this for a crowd, because you should eat it straight away and two soles are about all that will fit into the average skillet. But it is ideal for a tête-à-tête, weekday or otherwise, when you need something elegant and satisfying, in no time at all. Serve with a nice dry French white wine such as a Chablis.

2–3 tablespoons all-purpose flour

2 fresh sole, about 10 oz. each, skinned and cleaned

2 tablespoons safflower oil

4 tablespoons unsalted butter

fine sea salt

freshly squeezed juice of ½ a lemon

a handful of flat-leaf parsley, finely chopped

lemon slices, to serve

Serves 2

Put the flour on a large plate, add the fish, cover with flour on both sides, and shake off the excess.

Heat the oil and all but 2 tablespoons of the butter over medium-high heat in a nonstick skillet large enough to hold both fish side by side. When it sizzles, add the sole and cook for about 3 minutes. Turn them over and cook on the other side for 3 minutes. Sprinkle the first side with salt while the second side is cooking.

When the fish is cooked through, transfer to warmed serving plates and season the second side.

Return the skillet to the heat, add the remaining butter and melt over high heat. When it begins to sizzle, lower the heat and add the lemon juice. Cook, scraping the pan for about 10 seconds; do not let the butter burn. Pour the sauce over the fish and sprinkle with parsley. Serve immediately, garnished with thin slices of lemon.

Roughly translated, the English version of this dish means "roast from the sea." A gigot is the leg, usually of lamb, but here it refers to the sturdy, meaty nature of monkfish. Most other fish would be overwhelmed by the robust flavors in this Provençal preparation. There is certainly nothing fishy about this, which makes it ideal for those who are less than enthusiastic about eating food from the sea. Good fishmongers will make sure the thin grey membrane that lies under the skin is removed; but if it isn't, insist that it is, all the way down the tail, because it's a difficult job to do at home.

Whole roast monkfish   Gigot de mer

1 monkfish tail, about 1 lb. 5 oz.

about 12 thin slices smoked bacon, pancetta, or prosciutto (enough to cover the fish)

2 tablespoons olive oil

1½ cups mushrooms, sliced

2 large garlic cloves, crushed

1 cup dry white wine

2 lbs. tomatoes, skinned, seeded, and chopped

2 tablespoons crème fraîche or sour cream

a handful of basil leaves, chopped

coarse sea salt and freshly ground black pepper

a large baking dish

Serves 4

Preheat the oven to 425°F.

Put the bacon on a work surface with the slices slightly overlapping each other. Lay the monkfish on top, belly up. Wrap it in the bacon with the ends overlapping across the belly. Turn it over, cover, and set aside.

Heat the oil in a large skillet. Add the mushrooms and a pinch of salt and cook for 3–5 minutes, until browned. Stir in the garlic, then add the wine and cook over high heat for 1 minute. Stir in the tomatoes, salt lightly, and simmer gently for 5 minutes.

Pour the tomato sauce into a baking dish just large enough to hold the fish. Set the fish on top and roast in the preheated oven for 15 minutes. Lower the temperature to 400°F and roast for 30 minutes more. Remove from the oven and transfer the fish to a plate. Stir the crème fraîche and basil into the tomato sauce. Put the monkfish back on top and serve.

Sea bass and fennel are virtually inseparable in Provençal cuisine. The market fish stalls of the south always have a plentiful supply of gleaming silvery bass, and fennel grows wild all over the countryside, so it's no wonder. Saffron and harissa, a spicy Moroccan chile paste, are not traditional, but recipes and ingredients from the former French colonies in North Africa are now found all over France, especially in the south. Serve with a Bandol rosé.

Braised sea bass and fennel with saffron and harissa Bar braisé au fenouil epicé

3 tablespoons olive oil

1 onion, thinly sliced

3 large fennel bulbs, quartered and thinly sliced

2 cups fresh fish stock

a large pinch of saffron threads

8 oz. red potatoes, peeled and cut into large chunks

2 small fresh sea bass, cleaned, scaled, and heads removed if preferred

1–2 teaspoons harissa paste

coarse sea salt and freshly ground black pepper

Serves 2

Heat the oil in a large sauté pan with a lid. Add the onion and fennel and cook for about 5 minutes, until lightly golden brown. Season with a little salt. Add the fish stock and saffron, cover, and simmer gently for 15 minutes.

Meanwhile, put the potatoes in a large saucepan with sufficient water to cover and boil for 15–20 minutes, until tender. Drain, coarsely crush with a fork, and set aside.

Season the fish inside and out. Put it on top of the fennel, cover, and simmer gently for 10–15 minutes, until the fish is cooked through.

Remove the fish from the pan, set them on large serving plates and keep them warm in a low oven. Increase the heat and cook the fennel mixture over high heat for 5 minutes. Add the crushed potatoes and harissa and continue cooking, covered, for about 5 minutes more, until warmed through. Taste and adjust the seasoning, then spoon onto the plates beside the fish and serve.

*VARIATION Replace the crushed potatoes with couscous, but serve alongside the fish and vegetables instead of mixing it in; stir the harissa into the fennel before serving.

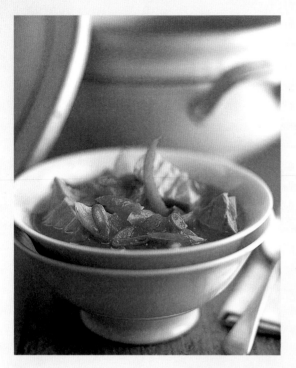

Tuna stew with chiles and potatoes

Thon marmitako

A traditional fish dish from the Basque region, where tuna abounds and chiles are appreciated more than in other parts of France. This is quick to prepare and doesn't require long simmering, perfect when you want something hearty and full of flavor in about an hour.

⅓ cup olive oil

2 onions, sliced

3 green bell peppers, halved, seeded, and sliced

3 red bell peppers, halved, seeded, and sliced

1½ lbs. red tuna steaks, cut into 2-inch pieces

3 large, hot green chiles, seeded and sliced

4 ripe tomatoes, skinned, seeded, and chopped

4 garlic cloves, crushed

2 lbs. new potatoes, peeled and cut into wedges

750-ml bottle dry white wine

coarse sea salt and freshly ground black pepper

baguette, to serve

Serves 4

Heat the oil in a large heavy-based saucepan. Add the onions and bell peppers and cook over high heat for 3–5 minutes, until brown. Transfer to a bowl and season with salt and pepper.

Add the tuna and chiles to the pan and cook for 3–5 minutes, just to sear. Add the tomatoes, garlic, and potatoes and salt to taste and stir carefully.

Return the onion mixture to the pan and pour in the wine. Add 1 cup water. Bring to a boil and boil for 1 minute, then reduce the heat, cover, and simmer gently for 30–35 minutes, until the potatoes are cooked through. Serve immediately with crusty baguette.

Mussels with fennel, tomatoes, garlic, and saffron   Moules à la bouillabaisse

Large bowls of steaming hot mussels are enjoyed all over France. The classic recipe is à la marinière, with shallots and white wine. My combination of ingredients evolved because I could eat mussels every day, just steamed plain, but not everyone shares my enthusiasm for them served this way. If, however, they come in a garlicky, saffron-scented sauce, reminiscent of summer holidays, then most people are happy.

2 tablespoons olive oil

1 small onion, chopped

½ fennel bulb, chopped

4 garlic cloves, crushed

1 cup dry white wine

2 cups canned chopped tomatoes

a pinch of saffron threads

2 lbs. fresh mussels

a handful of flat-leaf parsley, chopped

coarse sea salt and freshly ground black pepper

baguette, to serve

Serves 4

Heat the oil in a large sauté pan. Add the onion and fennel and cook for 3–5 minutes, until soft. Add the garlic, wine, and tomatoes. Boil for 1 minute, then reduce the heat, add the saffron and a pinch of salt. Simmer gently for 15 minutes.

Clean and debeard the mussels, discarding any that do not close. (To prepare mussels, see note on page 33.) Increase the heat under the sauce and, when boiling, add the prepared mussels. Cover and cook for 2–3 minutes, until the mussels open. Discard any that do not open. Sprinkle with parsley and serve immediately with crusty baguette.

*VARIATION Frites are the classic accompaniments for mussels when served as a main course. See the recipe on page 44.

Le grand aiöli

Salt cod and snails are traditional ingredients in this Provençal dish, but salmon and shrimp are easier to come by for most people. Be sure to use very good oil; despite great quantities of garlic, the flavor base of the aiöli comes from the oil, so it is worth investing in something special. Serve for a crowd, with everything freshly cooked and warmish, or at room temperature. Wash it all down with a chilled white or rosé from Provence.

10 oz. small new potatoes
4 tablespoons olive oil
4 fresh salmon steaks
8 oz. unpeeled shrimp tails
5 oz. asparagus tips
1 fresh bay leaf
6 baby carrots, sliced lengthwise
1 cauliflower, broken into florets
1 broccoli, broken into florets
8 oz. baby zucchini, halved
    lengthwise
6 eggs
8 oz. fine green beans
6 oz. cherry tomatoes
4 cooked beets
coarse sea salt

Aiöli

2 egg yolks
about 1⅓ cups extra virgin olive oil
6 large garlic cloves
fine sea salt

Serves 6

To make the aiöli, put the egg yolks in a small, deep bowl. Whisk well, then gradually whisk in the oil, adding it a little at a time and whisking vigorously, until the mixture is as thick as mayonnaise. Stir in the garlic and season to taste. Cover and set aside.

Put the potatoes in a saucepan with sufficient salted water to cover, bring to a boil and cook for 10–15 minutes, until tender. Drain and set aside.

Meanwhile, heat 1 tablespoon of the oil in a nonstick skillet, add the salmon steaks, and cook for about 3 minutes on each side, until just cooked through. Season and set aside. Heat another 1 tablespoon of the oil in the same pan. Add the shrimp and cook for 3–5 minutes, until pink and firm. Season and set aside.

Bring a saucepan of salted water to a boil and cook the asparagus tips and beans for about 3 minutes, until just tender. Drain and set aside.

Bring another saucepan of water to a boil with the bay leaf. Add the carrots and cook for 3–4 minutes, until just tender. Remove with a slotted spoon and set aside. Return the water to a boil, add the cauliflower and cook for about 5 minutes, until just tender. Remove with a slotted spoon and set aside. Return the water to a boil, add the broccoli and cook for 3–4 minutes, until just tender. Set aside.

Rub the zucchini all over with the remaining oil. Heat a ridged stovetop grill pan. When hot, add the zucchini slices and cook for about 4 minutes on each side. (Alternatively, cook in a nonstick skillet.) Season and set aside.

Put the eggs in a saucepan with sufficient water to cover. Bring to a boil and cook for 6 minutes from boiling point. Cool under running water, peel, and slice.

Arrange all of the ingredients on a single platter and serve with the aiöli.

Simple dishes

Ratatouille

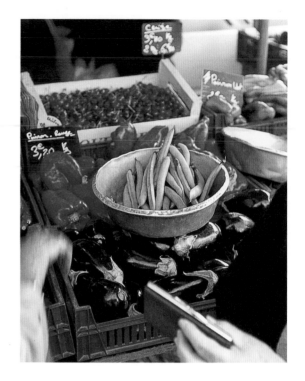

I first learned to make ratatouille from a friend's mother in her kitchen in Aix-en-Provence. Her method involves adding each vegetable separately, in the order which best suits their cooking requirements. It does make a difference because I've rarely tasted a ratatouille as good. It is also important to season each vegetable "layer" individually. Finally, I prefer my ratatouille vegetables to be distinct from each another, so cut the pieces medium-large, about 1½ inches. Serve with crusty bread.

2 lbs. eggplant, cut into pieces

extra virgin olive oil (see method)

2 medium onions, coarsely chopped

2 red bell peppers, halved, seeded, and cut into pieces

2 yellow bell peppers, halved, seeded, and cut into pieces

1 green bell pepper, halved, seeded, and cut into pieces

6 small zucchini, about 1½ lbs., halved lengthways and sliced

5 garlic cloves, crushed

6 tomatoes, halved, seeded, and chopped

leaves from a small bunch of basil, coarsely chopped, plus a few extra shredded, to serve

coarse sea salt

a large flameproof casserole dish

Serves 4—6

Put the eggplant pieces in a microwave-proof bowl with 3 tablespoons water and microwave on HIGH for 6 minutes. Drain and set aside.

Heat 3 tablespoons of the oil in a large flameproof casserole dish. Add the onions and cook for 3–5 minutes, until soft. Salt lightly.

Add all the bell peppers and cook for 5–8 minutes more, stirring often. Turn up the heat to keep the sizzling sound going, but take care not to let it burn. Salt lightly.

Add 1 more tablespoon of the oil and the zucchini. Mix well and cook for about 5 minutes more, stirring occasionally. Salt lightly.

Add 2 more tablespoons of the oil and the drained eggplants. Cook, stirring often, for 5 minutes more. Salt lightly.

Add 4 of the crushed garlic cloves and cook for 1 minute. Add 1 more tablespoon of the oil if necessary, and the tomatoes and chopped basil and stir well. Salt lightly. Cook for 5 minutes, then cover, reduce the heat and simmer gently for 30 minutes, checking occasionally.

Remove from the heat. Stir in the remaining garlic clove and shredded basil just before serving. This is best served at room temperature, but it still tastes nice hot. The longer you let it stand, the richer it tastes.

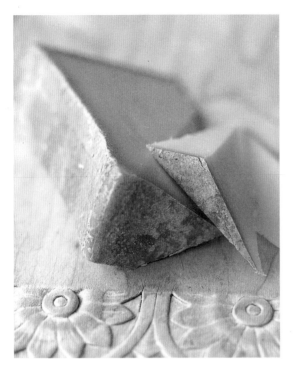

This bistro classic is a much more sophisticated version of macaroni and cheese. It is ideal for serving with beef stews, as the gratin is even better when mixed with broth.

Macaroni gratin   Gratin de macaroni

10 oz. macaroni

2 cups milk

3 tablespoons crème fraîche or sour cream

4 tablespoons unsalted butter

¼ cup all-purpose flour

1⅔ cups finely grated Beaufort cheese* (about 7 oz.)

coarse sea salt and freshly ground black pepper

a baking dish, 12 inches long, greased with butter

Serves 6

Cook the macaroni according to the package instructions. Drain, rinse well, and return to the empty saucepan.

Heat the milk in a saucepan and stir in the crème fraîche. Melt the butter in a separate saucepan set over medium-high heat. Stir in the flour and cook, stirring constantly, for 3 minutes. Pour in the milk mixture and stir constantly until the mixture thickens. Season with salt and pepper.

Preheat the broiler. Stir the milk mixture into the macaroni and taste, adding more salt and pepper if necessary. Transfer to the prepared baking dish and sprinkle with the cheese. Cook under the preheated broiler for 10–15 minutes, until bubbling and browned. Serve hot.

*NOTE Beaufort is an alpine cheese, similar to Gruyère, but with a slightly sweeter, more pronounced nutty flavor. It is becoming more widely available outside France, my local supermarket always has some, but if you cannot find it, Emmental, Cantal or any firm, Cheddar-like cheese will do. The taste will be entirely different, of course.

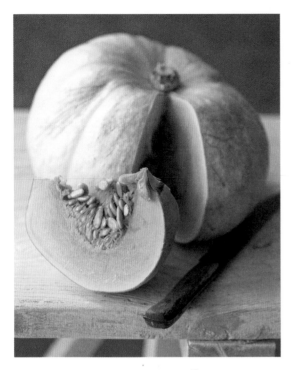

Though pumpkin is not usually associated with French cooking, it is in fact a very traditional ingredient. In the south of France, when it is in season, it is often enjoyed as a gratin. The conventional recipe is simply a purée with béchamel and a topping of crisp, browned bread crumbs. This version has rice, which gives it a more interesting texture and makes it substantial enough to be a meal on its own, served with a green salad.

Pumpkin and rice gratin Gratin de courge et de riz

3 lbs. pumpkin

3 tablespoons olive oil

½ cup long grain rice

a sprig of thyme

3 tablespoons fresh bread crumbs

a small handful of flat-leaf parsley, finely chopped

3 tablespoons crème fraîche or sour cream

¾ cup finely grated Gruyère cheese

coarse sea salt and freshly ground black pepper

a large baking dish, greased with butter

Serves 6

Peel and deseed the pumpkin and cut it into small cubes. Put in a large saucepan with 2 tablespoons of the oil, a pinch of salt, and 1 cup water. Cook over low heat for 20–30 minutes, stirring often, until soft and adding more water as necessary.

Meanwhile, put the rice and the remaining 1 tablespoon oil in a separate saucepan and cook over medium heat, stirring to coat the grains. Add 1 cup water, the thyme, and a pinch of salt and bring to a boil. Cover and simmer for 10 minutes, until almost tender. Drain and discard the thyme.

Preheat the oven to 400°F. Mix the bread crumbs with the parsley and a pinch of salt. Set aside.

Mash the cooked pumpkin into a coarse purée with a wooden spoon and stir in the cooked rice and crème fraîche. Taste; the topping and cheese will add flavor, but the pumpkin mixtue should be seasoned as well.

Spoon the pumpkin mixture into the prepared baking dish, spreading evenly. Sprinkle the cheese over the top, then follow with the bread crumbs. Bake in the preheated oven for 20–30 minutes, until browned. Serve hot.

Eggplant, onion, and tomato tian

Tian d'aubergines aux oignons et tomates

Tian is the Provençal name for a square earthenware baking dish, but I use a nonstick roasting pan and the tian still tastes great. Ideally, it should be served tepid or at room temperature, as it would be for the sweltering heat of a Provençal summer. The tian will improve with age and can easily be made one day in advance.

4 medium eggplants, sliced
  crossways into 1-inch pieces

5 tablespoons fresh bread crumbs

½ teaspoon dried herbes
  de provence

about ½ cup olive oil

2 large onions, sliced into
  thick rings

3 large tomatoes, sliced

¼ cup pitted black olives, sliced

coarse sea salt and freshly ground
  black pepper

Tomato sauce

1 tablespoon olive oil

3 garlic cloves

3 lbs. tomatoes, skinned, seeded,
  and chopped

a pinch of sugar

a small handful of basil, chopped

a small handful of flat-leaf parsley,
  chopped

coarse sea salt and freshly ground
  black pepper

*a nonstick roasting pan or
  rectangular baking dish*

Serves 4—6

Preheat the oven to 400°F.

To make the tomato sauce, heat the oil in a saucepan, add the garlic and cook for 1–2 minutes, until just soft. Add the tomatoes, sugar and salt to taste. Cover and simmer gently for 10 minutes. Stir in the basil and parsley and set aside.

Bring a large saucepan of water to a boil and add a pinch of salt. Add the eggplant slices and cook for 3–5 minutes, until just blanched and tender. Drain well.

Put the bread crumbs, dried herbs, and a pinch of salt in a bowl, mix well and set aside.

Pour 3–4 tablespoons of the oil into the baking dish, arrange the eggplant rounds on top and drizzle with some of the remaining oil. Top with the onion rings and sprinkle with salt and pepper. Dot the tomato sauce on top, spreading as evenly as possible. Arrange the tomato slices on top, sprinkle with the bread crumbs, followed by the olives. Bake in the preheated oven for about 45 minutes, until well browned. Serve hot or warm.

Potatoes with reblochon Tartiflette

A meal in itself, this is very rich and filling, just the sort of thing to serve after a day on the ski slopes. You might find this on menus in the Savoie region of France, though it is not, strictly speaking, a traditional recipe. It was "invented" in the 1980s by the local cheese committee to help sell more Reblochon cheese—and I'm sold! Serve with a salad greens and a bottle of chilled vin d'Aprémont from the Savoie, which is what you should use in the cooking.

2¼ lbs. waxy salad-style potatoes
1 fresh bay leaf
4 tablespoons unsalted butter
2 onions, halved and sliced
5 oz. bacon lardons
⅓ cup dry white wine
1-lb. Reblochon cheese*
coarse sea salt and freshly
ground black pepper

a baking dish, about 12 inches long, greased with butter

Serves 6

Put the potatoes in a large saucepan, then add the bay leaf and sufficient cold water to cover. Bring to a boil, add a generous pinch of salt, and cook for about 15 minutes, until the potatoes are just tender. Drain. When cool enough to handle, peel and slice.

Melt half the butter in a sauté pan, add the onions and bacon lardons and cook until just browned. Remove with a slotted spoon and set aside. Add the remaining butter to the pan with the potatoes and cook gently for 5 minutes. Stir carefully without breaking too many potato slices. Add the wine, bring to a boil, and boil for 1 minute. Season with salt and pepper.

Preheat the oven to 425°F. Arrange the potatoes in the prepared baking dish. Spoon the onions and bacon on top of the potatoes. Scrub the rind of the cheese lightly with a vegetable brush, then cut into 8 wedges. Cut each piece in half through the middle, so each has skin on one side only. Put the cheese on top of the potatoes, skin-side up. Cover with foil and bake in the preheated oven for 15 minutes. Remove the foil and bake for 15–20 minutes more, until browned. Serve hot.

*NOTE If Reblochon is unavailable, substitute any other French mountain cheese, such as Emmental, Cantal, or a Pyrénées. A firm goat cheese such as Crottin de Chavignol, is also very nice. Alternatively, this recipe is a great way to clear out a cluttered cheese compartment, especially the post-dinner party syndrome of lovely but unfinished cheeses. Simply crumble or slice whatever you've got and arrange it on top of the potatoes before baking.

Salads and sides

Mixed leaf salad with garlic vinaigrette

Salade verte, vinaigrette à l'ail

Green salads do not appear as often on French menus as an appetizer or side dish as they do in other countries, though they are still served in very traditional bistros. Home is the main place for eating salads, and they're eaten daily, usually after the entrée and either before or with a cheese course. Raw garlic is not always included, but the vinaigrette method is classic, the way I was taught to make it when I first moved to France, and the way I've made it ever since.

2 tablespoons wine vinegar

½ teaspoon fine sea salt

1 teaspoon Dijon mustard

6 tablespoons olive oil

2 garlic cloves, crushed

freshly ground white pepper

8 oz. tender, mixed salad leaves, washed and dried

a handful of flat-leaf parsley, coarsely chopped

a small bunch of chives, snipped

Serves 4

Put the vinegar in a salad bowl. Using a fork or a small whisk, stir in the salt until almost dissolved. You may have to tilt the bowl so the vinegar is deep enough to have something to stir around.

Stir in the mustard until completely blended. Add the oil, a tablespoon at a time, whisking well between each addition, until emulsified. Mix in the garlic and add pepper to taste.

If you like a powerful garlic punch, add the salad leaves to the bowl with the parsley and chives, then toss and serve immediately. I prefer to let the garlic sit in the dressing for at least 30 minutes to mellow it a bit. In any case, do not add the salad greens until you are ready to serve or they will become soggy.

Tomato salad with anchovy vinaigrette

Salade de tomates, vinaigrette à l'anchoïade

Anchoïade is a Provençal anchovy paste, which is spread thickly on grilled bread slices or served with raw vegetables as an appetizer. Here it becomes a dressing for what will hopefully be very ripe, flavorful tomatoes. If these are not available, use boiled baby new potatoes instead and toss while the potatoes are still warm. Serve with a chilled Provençal rosé and lots of crusty bread.

1½ lbs. ripe vine tomatoes
1 large shallot, or 1 small red onion, thinly sliced
coarse sea salt and freshly ground black pepper

Anchovy vinaigrette

1 garlic clove
½ teaspoon Dijon mustard
2 tablespoons white wine vinegar
6 anchovy fillets, packed in oil
8 tablespoons extra virgin olive oil
a small handful of basil leaves
a handful of flat-leaf parsley, finely chopped
freshly ground black pepper
crusty bread, to serve

Serves 4

To make the vinaigrette, put the garlic, mustard, vinegar, and anchovies in a small food processor and blend well. Add the oil, 1 tablespoon at a time, then blend in the basil, reserving a few leaves. Season with pepper and set aside.

Cut the tomatoes into quarters or eighths, depending on their size. Arrange on a plate and sprinkle with the sliced shallot. Season lightly with salt, then spoon the dressing over the top. Sprinkle with the parsley, reserved basil leaves, and freshly ground black pepper. Serve at room temperature with crusty bread.

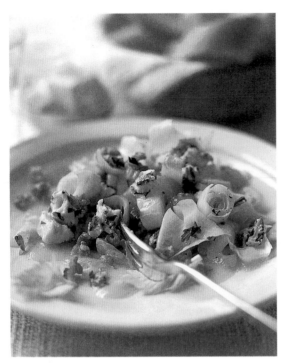

Mine is a family of serial salad eaters, but I'd never heard of Belgian endive until moving to France. In those days, it was still a fairly bitter thing, available only in winter and an acquired taste, but it has come a long way. Developed unintentionally by a gardener at the Brussels botanical gardens in the middle of the nineteenth century, endive is now cultivated for a good part of the year, and modern varieties have none of the bitterness of their ancestors. When buying, choose very pale endives with only a hint of green; they grow in the dark, so color on the leaves is a sign that they have been exposed to the light and are not as fresh.

Belgian endive salad with roquefort, celery, and walnuts Salade d'endives aux roquefort, céleri et noix

4–5 heads of Belgian endive, about 1¼ lbs., halved, cored, and thinly sliced

2 celery ribs, thinly sliced, plus a few leaves, torn

3 oz. Roquefort cheese, crumbled

⅓ cup shelled walnuts, chopped

a handful of flat-leaf parsley, finely chopped

crusty bread, to serve

Walnut vinaigrette

2 tablespoons wine vinegar

1 teaspoon fine sea salt

1 teaspoon Dijon mustard

7 tablespoons safflower oil (see method)

1 tablespoon walnut oil (optional)

freshly ground white pepper

To prepare the vinaigrette, put the vinegar in a salad bowl. Using a fork or a small whisk, stir in the salt until almost dissolved. You may have to tilt the bowl so the vinegar is deep enough to have something to stir.

Mix in the mustard until completely blended. Add the oil, a tablespoon at a time, beating well between each addition, until emulsified. If you're using the walnut oil, use one less tablespoon of safflower oil. Add pepper to taste.

Just before you're ready to serve the salad, add the Belgian endive, celery, Roquefort, walnuts, and parsley and toss well. Serve immediately, with plenty of crusty bread.

Serves 4

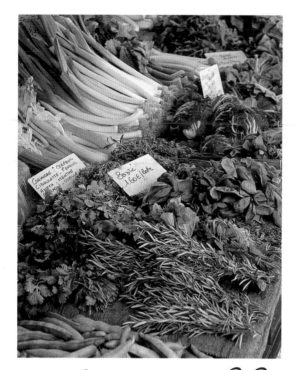

Lovely leeks are delicious with this lively herb-studded sauce. Serve at the start of a substantial spread, to allow room for expansion, or as part of a light lunch with the Goat Cheese Tart on page 19. If you can't find sorrel, it will be a shame, but the recipe works without, so don't feel obliged to replace it with anything.

Baby leeks with herb vinaigrette

Poireaux, vinaigrette aux herbes

1½ lbs. baby leeks
¼ cup wine vinegar
1 teaspoon Dijon mustard
1 teaspoon fine sea salt
1 cup safflower oil
a small handful of flat-leaf parsley
a small handful of watercress
a small handful of tarragon
3 sorrel leaves
2 shallots, thinly sliced
a small bunch of chives, snipped
freshly ground black pepper

Serves 4

Put the leeks in the top of a steamer and cook for about 7–10 minutes, until tender. Remove and set aside to drain.

To make the vinaigrette, put the vinegar, mustard, and salt in a small food processor and blend well. Add about ⅓ cup of the oil and blend for a few seconds. Continue adding the oil, a little at a time, and blending until the vinaigrette is emulsified. Add the parsley, watercress, tarragon, and sorrel and pulse again to chop. Add pepper to taste. (Alternatively, see page 101 for the hand-mixing method, and you'll have to chop all the herbs finely.)

If the leeks are still too wet, pat dry with paper towels. Arrange the leeks in a serving dish, spoon the vinaigrette over the top, and sprinkle with shallot slices and chives. Serve with any remaining vinaigrette on the side.

Poor old celery; it is more often an ingredient than the star of a dish. However, in this traditional Provençal recipe, it takes center stage. Beef is the ideal complement to the trinity of celery, tomatoes, and anchovies, so serve this with roast beef or grilled steaks.

Braised celery Céleri braisé

2 whole bunches of celery

2 tablespoons olive oil

3 oz. bacon lardons

1 onion, halved, then quartered and sliced

1 carrot, halved lengthwise, then quartered and sliced

2 garlic cloves, sliced

1 cup canned chopped tomatoes

1 cup dry white wine

1 fresh bay leaf

8 canned anchovy fillets, about 8, chopped

a handful of flat-leaf parsley, chopped

coarse sea salt and freshly ground black pepper

Serves 4—6

Remove any tough outer sticks from the celery and trim the tips so they will just fit into a large sauté pan with a lid.

Bring a large saucepan of water to a boil. Add a pinch of salt, then the celery and simmer gently for 10 minutes to blanch. Remove, drain, and pat dry with paper towels.

Heat the oil in the sauté pan. Add the bacon lardons, onion, and carrot and cook gently until lightly browned. Add the celery and a little salt and pepper and cook just to brown, then remove.

Add the garlic, cook for 1 minute, then add the tomatoes, wine, and bay leaf. Bring to a boil and cook for 1 minute. Add the celery, cover, and simmer gently for 30 minutes, turning the celery once during cooking.

Transfer the celery to a serving dish. Increase the heat and cook the sauce for about 10 minutes, to reduce it slightly. Pour it over the celery, sprinkle with the anchovies and parsley and serve.

Carrots with cream and herbs

Carottes à la crème aux herbes

Thyme is omnipresent in French cuisine. Here, it transforms what would otherwise be ordinary boiled carrots into something subtly sumptuous. The crème fraîche helps too. You can substitute steamed baby leeks for the carrots, but stir in a tablespoon or so of butter when adding the crème fraîche.

2 lbs. mini carrots, trimmed, or medium carrots
3 tablespoons unsalted butter
a sprig of thyme
2 tablespoons crème fraîche or sour cream
several sprigs of chervil, snipped
a small bunch of chives, snipped
fine sea salt

Serves 4

If using larger carrots, cut them diagonally into 2-inch slices. Put in a large saucepan (the carrots should fit in almost a single layer for even cooking.) Add the butter and set over low heat. Cook for 3 minutes, until the butter has melted and coated the carrots. Half fill the saucepan with water, then add a pinch of salt and the thyme. Cover and cook for 10–20 minutes, until the water is almost completely evaporated.

Stir in the crème fraîche and add salt to taste. Sprinkle the chervil and chives over the top, mix well and serve.

French beans with garlic

Haricots verts à l'ail

French beans are a classic accompaniment for lamb, but they are equally nice with fish and chicken. You can also serve at room temperature, as part of a salad buffet. Instead of the cooked beans, try long, thin slices of steamed zucchini, sautéed with the garlic.

1½ lbs. fine green beans, trimmed
2 tablespoons olive oil
1 tablespoon unsalted butter
2 garlic cloves, crushed
a handful of flat-leaf parsley, chopped
1 teaspoon freshly squeezed lemon juice
sea salt and freshly ground black pepper

Serves 4

Bring a large saucepan of water to a boil. Add the beans and cook for 3–4 minutes from the time the water returns to a boil. Drain and refresh under cold running water. Set aside.

Heat the oil and butter in a sauté pan. Add the garlic, beans, and salt, and cook on high for 1 minute, stirring. Remove from the heat and stir in the parsley and lemon juice. Sprinkle with pepper and serve.

CORIANDRE · CERFEUIL
CIBOULETTE · FENOUIL
ANETH · MENTHE
ESTRAGON ·

Basilic
1.60€/Botte

Spinach flan Flan d'épinards

Years ago, I went on a wine-buying mission with some friends in the Jura region of France. We stopped for lunch at a small hotel, but it was very late in the day, so we had to take what we were given. The offering was roast pork, served with a glorious mixture of vegetables, all thinly sliced and baked in a fabulous savory custard. Back home, I tried a similar dish using just spinach, because that's what was on hand, and it proved a great success.

1 lb. fresh spinach
3–5 tablespoons olive oil
¾ cup crème fraîche or sour cream
2 eggs
1 teaspoon coarse sea salt
a pinch of freshly grated nutmeg
1 tablespoon unsalted butter

a baking dish, 12 inches long

Serves 4

Preheat the oven to 350°F.

Wash the spinach, then spin-dry in a salad spinner. Working in batches, heat 1 tablespoon of the oil in a nonstick sauté pan and add a mound of spinach. Cook the spinach over high heat, stirring until all the leaves have just wilted. Transfer to a plastic colander and let drain. Continue cooking until all the spinach has been wilted.

Chop the spinach coarsely. Put the crème fraîche, eggs, salt, and nutmeg in a bowl and whisk well. Stir in the spinach.

Spread the butter in the bottom of a baking dish. Transfer the spinach mixture to the dish and bake in the preheated oven for 25–30 minutes, until just set. Serve hot.

Peas, asparagus, and baby lettuce

Petits pois, asperges, et laitues à la française

Freshly shelled peas with lettuce form one of the classics of French cuisine. Teamed with asparagus in a light buttery sauce, they're ideal for serving with roast poultry or grilled fish. Bacon makes a nice addition so stir in about ¼ cup finely chopped sautéed bacon, just before serving, if liked.

6 tablespoons unsalted butter

3–4 shallots, sliced into rounds

2 romaine lettuce hearts, quartered

4 oz. asparagus tips, halved

2 cups shelled fresh peas (about 2 lbs. in the pod)

coarse sea salt

sprigs of chervil or flat-leaf parsley, finely chopped, or chives, snipped, to serve

Serves 4

Melt half the butter in a saucepan with a lid. Add the shallots and lettuce and cover. Cook, stirring often, for 8–10 minutes, until tender. Season with salt, add the remaining butter and the asparagus, cover, and cook for 5 minutes more. Add the peas, cover, and cook for 3 minutes more. Taste for seasoning, sprinkle with the herbs and serve.

　*Variation For a more substantial side dish, or even a light meal, add 10 oz. sliced baby carrots and a splash of water when cooking the lettuce. Before serving, gently stir in more butter or 1 tablespoon crème fraîche and add 1 lb. boiled small new potatoes, sliced into wedges.

This classic recipe goes especially well with pork. The secret of delicious cauliflower is to blanch it first; if you parboil it with a bay leaf, the unpleasant cabbage aroma disappears.

Cauliflower gratin Gratin de chou-fleur

1 large cauliflower, separated
  into large florets

1 fresh bay leaf

2 cups heavy cream

1 egg

2 teaspoons Dijon mustard

1½ cups grated Comté cheese*
  (about 6 oz.)

coarse sea salt

*a baking dish, about 10 inches
diameter, greased with butter*

Serves 4—6

Bring a large saucepan of water to a boil, add the bay leaf, salt generously, then add the cauliflower florets. Cook for about 10 minutes, until still slightly firm. Drain and set aside.

Put the cream in a saucepan and bring to a boil. Boil for 10 minutes. Add a spoonful of hot milk to the beaten egg to warm it, then stir the egg, mustard, and 1 teaspoon salt into the cream.

Preheat the oven to 400°F. Divide the cauliflower into smaller florets, then stir them into the cream sauce. Transfer to the prepared baking dish and sprinkle the cheese over the top in an even layer.

Bake in the preheated oven for 40–45 minutes, until golden. Serve hot.

*NOTE Like Gruyère, Comté is a mountain cheese—from the Franche-Comté region to be precise—but the similarity stops there. Comté's distinct flavor comes from the milk used in the making, so the flavor varies with the seasons. A springtime diet of tender young shoots delivers milk that is very different from its winter counterpart, nourished mainly on hay. I've never met a Comté I didn't like, but it is darker in color and fruitier in summer, paler and more nutty in winter. Use Emmental or Cantal if it is unavailable.

Braised red cabbage with chestnuts and apples
Chou rouge aux marrons et aux pommes

There are several regional variations on this recipe and it was difficult to choose which one to include. Chou rouge à la flammande has apples, à la limousine has chestnuts. This recipe has it all, with some Alsatian Riesling and bacon as well—serve it with grilled sausages, pork chops, or roasts, and the same wine as used in the cooking. It is also fantastic with Christmas goose.

1 red cabbage

3 tablespoons unsalted butter

1 onion, halved and thinly sliced

3 oz. bacon lardons

3 cooking apples, peeled, cored, and chopped

7 oz. vacuum-packed whole peeled chestnuts

2 teaspoons coarse sea salt

1 cup dry white wine, preferably Riesling

1 tablespoon sugar

Serves 4—6

Cut the cabbage in quarters, then core and slice thinly.

Melt 2 tablespoons of the butter in a sauté pan. Add the onion and lardons and cook for about 3 minutes, until soft.

Add the remaining butter, the cabbage, apples, and chestnuts and stir well. Season with salt, then add the wine, sugar, and 1 cup water.

Bring to a boil, boil for 1 minute, then cover and simmer gently for about 45 minutes, until the cabbage is tender.

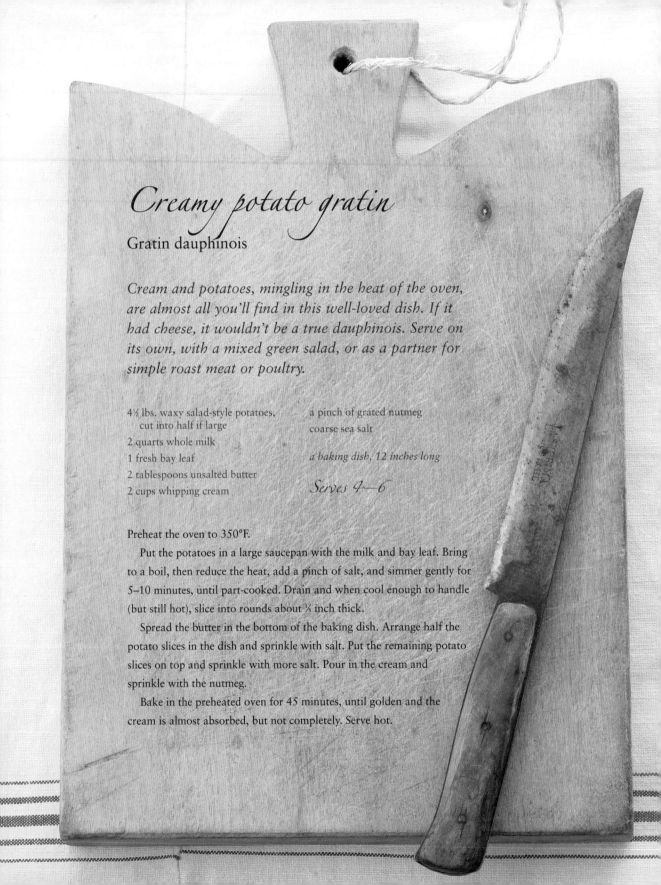

Creamy potato gratin
Gratin dauphinois

Cream and potatoes, mingling in the heat of the oven, are almost all you'll find in this well-loved dish. If it had cheese, it wouldn't be a true dauphinois. Serve on its own, with a mixed green salad, or as a partner for simple roast meat or poultry.

4½ lbs. waxy salad-style potatoes,
   cut into half if large
2 quarts whole milk
1 fresh bay leaf
2 tablespoons unsalted butter
2 cups whipping cream

a pinch of grated nutmeg
coarse sea salt

a baking dish, 12 inches long

Serves 4—6

Preheat the oven to 350°F.

   Put the potatoes in a large saucepan with the milk and bay leaf. Bring to a boil, then reduce the heat, add a pinch of salt, and simmer gently for 5–10 minutes, until part-cooked. Drain and when cool enough to handle (but still hot), slice into rounds about ⅛ inch thick.

   Spread the butter in the bottom of the baking dish. Arrange half the potato slices in the dish and sprinkle with salt. Put the remaining potato slices on top and sprinkle with more salt. Pour in the cream and sprinkle with the nutmeg.

   Bake in the preheated oven for 45 minutes, until golden and the cream is almost absorbed, but not completely. Serve hot.

Sweet things

Sugared strawberries   Fraises au sucre

As soon as it's strawberry season, you'll find this on menus all over France, though Plougastel in Brittany claims to be home to the best of the French strawberry crop. Wherever they come from, lemon juice is key, enhancing the flavor of the fruit as well as adding tartness to show off the sugar.

2 lbs. strawberries, at room
   temperature
freshly squeezed juice of 1 lemon
3–5 tablespoons sugar
crème fraîche, sour cream, or
   whipped cream, to serve

Serves 4—6

Trim the strawberries and put them in a pretty bowl. Add the lemon juice and 3 tablespoons of the sugar. Mix gently but thoroughly and let stand for about 15 minutes. Taste, and add more sugar if necessary.

This dish improves with standing, but don't leave it too long. If you make it just before you're ready to begin your meal, it will be ready in time for dessert.

If using crème fraîche, sweeten it with a spoonful of sugar.

*VARIATION Peach or nectarine slices can be substituted for the strawberries, if you like to stick to single fruit, or use a mixture of soft fruit including red currants, blueberries, raspberries, and blackberries.

Raspberry cream Crème aux framboises

I once stayed with a family in the Provençal village of Crest, where I remember having something similar made with fraise des bois (wild strawberries) and then again, with another family in Alsace, made with blueberries we had spent the afternoon gathering. But I also came across a recipe in an Elizabeth David book, which is what reminded me of its existence.

12 oz. raspberries, fresh or frozen and thawed, plus 1 small basket of fresh raspberries

5–6 tablespoons sugar, to taste

1 cup heavy cream, chilled

1 egg white

sprigs of mint, to serve

Serves 4

Put the raspberries in a blender or food processor and blend until smooth, then press through a strainer to obtain a smooth purée; you should have about 1 cup. Stir in 4–5 tablespoons of the sugar. Set aside.

Put the cream in a large bowl and beat with an electric mixer until it holds firm peaks. Set aside.

Beat the egg white with 1 tablespoon of the sugar until it holds firm peaks. Fold the beaten egg white and raspberry purée into the cream.

Divide the mixture between 4 serving glasses, filling half-way. Set aside 4 fresh raspberries, then divide the remaining fresh ones between the glasses and top with the remaining raspberry cream.

Decorate the top of each with a fresh raspberry and a mint sprig. Chill for up to 6 hours. Serve cold.

*VARIATION Use fromage frais in place of the heavy cream, or use half heavy cream and half fromage frais. This can also be made with strawberries or mixed berries, though you will have to adjust the sugar content. Sweeten the fruit purée gradually, tasting as you go, until it is to your liking.

You don't need any special equipment to make a really fantastic frozen dessert, as this recipe will prove. It is also easy, fast, and probably takes first place ahead of all the other recipes in this book. Hard to believe, but this is better than chocolate cake. You can also freeze it in individual silicone molds, but be sure to choose a shape that will allow for a meringue in the middle of each one.

Honey parfait with meringue and caramelized pistachios

Parfait meringué au miel et aux pistaches caramelisées

1 cup shelled pistachio nuts
¼ cup sugar
1¼ cups heavy cream, chilled
2 eggs, separated
scant ⅓ cup clear honey
8–10 mini meringues
   or 6–8 meringue nests

*a loaf tin or other
  freezerproof mold*

Serves 6

Put the pistachios and sugar in a nonstick saucepan. Cook over medium/high heat, stirring, until they begin to caramelize. Remove from the pan and let cool. Grind coarsely in a food processor or by putting between 2 sheets of parchment paper and crushing with a rolling pin.

Put the cream in a large bowl and beat until firm. Set aside. Put the egg yolks and honey in a second bowl, whisk well, then set aside. Put the egg whites in a third bowl and beat until they hold stiff peaks. Set aside.

Fold the egg yolk mixture into the cream until blended. Gently fold in the egg whites until just blended. Fold in the pistachios.

Spoon half the mixture into a freezerproof mold. Arrange the meringues on top in a single layer—nests may have to be broken up depending on size, but not too small, because you want big pieces of meringue in the finished dish. Cover with the remaining parfait mixture and smooth the top. Cover with plastic wrap and freeze for about 6–8 hours or overnight, until firm. Scoop into tall glasses to serve.

Poached peaches in vanilla syrup

Les pêches pochées au sirop vanillé

Poached peaches are a very simple and elegant way to end a heavy meal. To jazz it up a bit, serve the peaches with a fresh raspberry coulis and vanilla ice cream and, voilà, Peach Melba, the famous dessert created by Escoffier for the great soprano, Dame Nellie Melba.

½ cup sugar
1 vanilla bean, split lengthwise with a small sharp knife
6 peaches, ripe but not too soft
sweetened whipped cream, to serve

Serves 6

Put 6 cups water into a saucepan. Add the sugar and vanilla bean, bring just to a boil, then simmer gently.

Bring another saucepan of water to a boil. Make a criss-cross incision in the base of each peach and plunge it into the boiling water for 30 seconds. Remove with a slotted spoon. Using a small knife, peel off the skin. Transfer the peeled peaches to the sugar syrup as they are peeled. Cover with a round of parchment paper and poach for 15–25 minutes, until tender.

Remove the peaches from the syrup with a slotted spoon. Increase the heat under the saucepan and boil the syrup to reduce by half. Let cool.

Serve in small bowls, with some of the poaching liquid and a dollop of cream.

Poached pears in honey wine

Les poires pochées au vin et au miel

This is a classic recipe but you can also poach the pears in the same way as the peaches (left) and serve with a chocolate sauce and vanilla ice cream—also known as Poires Belle Hélène.

750-ml bottle fruity red wine
4 tablespoons clear honey
a pinch of ground cinnamon
6 pears, ripe but not too soft

Serves 6

Put the wine, honey, and cinnamon in a saucepan large enough to take all the pears in one layer, stems upward. (Don't add the pears yet.) Bring just to a boil, then simmer gently.

Using a vegetable peeler, peel the fruit, leaving the stems intact. Put into the poaching liquid, stems upward. Poach for 15–25 minutes, until tender. Remove from the syrup with a slotted spoon. Increase the heat and boil the liquid to reduce by half. Let cool. Serve in small bowls, with some of the honey wine spooned over the top.

Chocolate mousse   Mousse au chocolat

This is very easy to make and ideal for entertaining, since it should be made one day in advance. It is also deceptively rich, thanks to the egg yolks, which can be reduced in quantity or omitted altogether. It is important to use good-quality chocolate, but anything over 70 percent cocoa solids will be too much. In traditional bistros, chocolate mousse is often served in a single, large bowl and passed around the table for diners to help themselves, so if you're expecting a crowd, double the recipe and do the same.

7 oz. bittersweet chocolate, broken into pieces

2 tablespoons unsalted butter, cut into small pieces

1 vanilla bean, split lengthwise with a small sharp knife

3 eggs, separated

a pinch of salt

2 tablespoons sugar

sweetened crème fraîche, sour cream, or whipped cream, to serve (optional)

Serves 4

Put the chocolate in a glass bowl and melt in the microwave on HIGH for 40 seconds. Remove, stir, and repeat until almost completely melted. Remove, then stir in the butter. Using the tip of a small knife, scrape the black seeds from the vanilla bean into the chocolate. Add the egg yolks, stir, and set aside.

Using an electric mixer, beat the egg whites and salt until foaming. Continue beating and add the sugar. Beat on high until glossy and firm.

Carefully fold the whites into the chocolate with a rubber spatula until no more white specks can be seen.

Transfer the mousse to serving dishes and refrigerate for at least 6 hours, but overnight is best.

*NOTE If you don't have a microwave, put the chocolate in a bowl over a saucepan of simmering water—don't let the water touch the bottom of the bowl. Leave until melted, stirring occasionally.

Caramel custard Crème renversée au caramel

These are neither too sweet, nor too heavy; the perfect ending to a substantial meal. Preparation is simple but there are a few tricks to facilitate unmolding. First, don't use molds that are too deep (and don't overfill them.) Then, let the custards stand in the bain-marie for a good 15 minutes before removing them to cool completely. According to a reliable old French cookbook of mine, this allows the custard to settle and solidify, making it easier to turn out. Just before serving, run a knife around the inside edge, hold an upturned plate over the top, and flip over to release the custard.

3 cups whole milk

1 vanilla bean, split lengthwise with a small sharp knife

¾ cup plus 2 tablespoons sugar

5 eggs

a pinch of salt

8 ramekin dishes

a roasting pan, large enough to hold the ramekins

Serves 8

Put the milk, vanilla bean, and its seeds in a saucepan and bring to a boil over medium heat. Immediately remove from the heat, cover, and let stand while you make the caramel.

To make the caramel, put ½ cup of the sugar, the salt, and ¼ tablespoons water in a small heavy-based saucepan, preferably with a pouring lip. Heat until the sugar turns a deep caramel color, then remove from the heat. When it stops sizzling, pour carefully into the ramekins. Take care not to let the caramel come into contact with your skin; it is very hot. Set the ramekins in a roasting pan and add enough boiling water to come half-way up the sides—this is called a bain-marie. Set aside.

Add the remaining sugar and the salt to the saucepan of warm milk and stir until dissolved. Remove the vanilla bean.

Crack the eggs into another bowl and whisk until smooth. Pour the warm milk into the eggs and stir well. Ladle into the ramekins.

Preheat the oven to 350°F. Carefully transfer the bain-marie with the ramekins into the preheated oven and bake for about 20–25 minutes, until the custard is set and a knife inserted into the middle comes out clean. Serve at room temperature either in their ramekins or inverted onto a plate so the caramel forms a pool of sweet sauce.

This very old-fashioned recipe evokes cries of "oo-la, les petits pots ..." from French acquaintances of a certain age. It's the sort of thing an auntie would have made in the kitchen of her country house during the summer hols. And most respectable aunties would have had special little pots, about the size of espresso cups, solely for this purpose. You can also use regular crème brûlée ramekins. Good-quality chocolate is imperative for a good result.

Chocolate cream pots   Petits pots au chocolat

1 cup whole milk

1 cup heavy cream

3½ oz. bittersweet chocolate, with at least 70 percent cocoa solids, finely chopped

3 whole eggs plus 2 egg yolks

⅔ cup sugar

6 heatproof ramekins or similar

a baking dish, large enough to hold the ramekins

Serves 6

Put the milk and cream in a saucepan. Bring just to a boil and remove from the heat. Stir in the chocolate until melted.

Put the eggs, yolks, and sugar in a large bowl and mix well, but don't beat until frothy; the finished dish should be smooth on top and beating too much will make too many bubbles that mar the surface. Pour in the milk mixture and stir gently until just mixed.

Bring a kettle of water to a boil and preheat the oven to 350°F.

Set the ramekins in a baking dish. Ladle the chocolate mixture into each ramekin to fill well. Open the preheated oven, pull out the shelf, and set the baking dish with the ramekins on the shelf. Pour the boiling water into the dish to come about two-thirds up the sides of the ramekins. Carefully push the shelf back in.

Cook for 25–30 minutes, until just set and still a bit jiggly in the middle. Remove the dish from the oven, let stand 5 minutes, then remove the ramekins from the water bath. Let cool uncovered. Serve warm or at room temperature.

The sweet and frothy egg mixture spread on top of the fruit is called a sabayon, making this a very easy and elegant dessert. It is best when made with a bit of something alcoholic—I prefer Muscat de Beaumes de Venise. The recipe requires only a small amount of wine and the remainder is just the thing to drink with this dish—ideal for special occasions.

Berry gratin De fruits des bois

1¼ lbs. frozen mixed berries, thawed

5 egg yolks and 3 egg whites

⅓ cup sugar

1 tablespoon clear honey

½ cup sweet dessert wine or champagne (optional)

1–2 tablespoons confectioners' sugar

4 shallow, ovenproof gratin dishes

Serves 4

Divide the fruit between the gratin dishes. Preheat the broiler to high.

Bring a saucepan of water just to simmering point. Choose a heatproof bowl (glass is ideal) that will sit tightly on top of the saucepan. Put the egg yolks and sugar in the bowl and beat, off the heat, until blended. Transfer the bowl to the saucepan and continue beating (over the heat) for 2–4 minutes, until the mixture is thick and frothy. Don't let the water reach a boil. Whisk in the honey and wine if using, and remove from the heat.

Beat the egg whites in another bowl until they hold stiff peaks.

Gently fold the beaten whites into the warm yolk mixture until blended. Divide between the gratin dishes, spreading evenly to cover the fruit. Lightly sprinkle the top of each with a dusting of confectioners' sugar (this will help it to color nicely). Cook under the broiler for 1–2 minutes, until just browned (watch carefully because they will color quite quickly.) Serve immediately.

*VARIATION Use fresh berries when in season. Raspberries and strawberries are best, mixed or on their own.

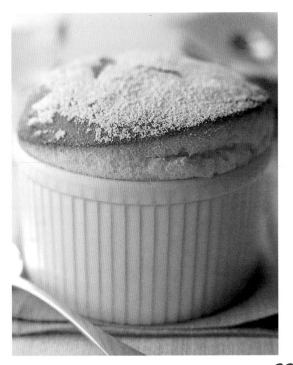

A lot of fuss is made about making soufflés, but it's really not that complicated. The main mixture can be prepared ahead of time, leaving you with nothing more than whisking egg whites and baking just before serving. It will inevitably fall as it cools, or when you stick a spoon in it, but this doesn't affect the taste in the slightest.

Vanilla orange soufflé Soufflé au vanille et à l'orange

1 cup whole milk

1 vanilla bean, split lengthwise with a small sharp knife

1 tablespoon finely grated orange peel

4 large egg yolks and 6 egg whites

½ cup sugar

3 tablespoons all-purpose flour

1 tablespoon Grand Marnier liqueur (optional)

a deep soufflé dish, about 6½ inches diameter, buttered and dusted with confectioners' sugar

Serves 4

Put the milk and vanilla bean in a saucepan set over medium heat. Bring just to a boil, then cover and set aside to infuse for 15 minutes.

Put the orange peel, egg yolks, and all but 1 tablespoon of the sugar in a large bowl and beat until slightly thickened and a paler yellow. Beat in the flour and the Grand Marnier, if using.

Scrape the vanilla seeds into the milk, then discard the bean. Gradually whisk the hot milk into the yolk mixture, then return to the saucepan and set over low heat. Cook for 2–3 minutes, stirring constantly with a wooden spoon, until thick enough to coat the back of the spoon. Let cool. (The recipe can be made up to 24 hours in advance to this stage, then cover and refrigerate until needed.)

Preheat the oven to 400°F.

Put the egg whites and remaining sugar in a separate bowl and beat until firm and glossy. Fold one-third of the egg whites into the cooled orange mixture until blended, then carefully but thoroughly fold in the rest.

Reduce the oven temperature to 350°F. Transfer the mixture to the prepared dish. Bake in the preheated oven for 20–30 minutes, until puffed. Serve immediately.

Chocolate and hazelnut soufflé cakes

Gâteaux moelleux au chocolat et aux noisettes

Though this recipe does require several mixing bowls, it is very easy to prepare. The effort will be worthwhile—these luscious little cakes are gooey and chocolatey and the perfect end to an elegant meal. Serve straight from the ramekins, pass around something creamy to pour or dollop and enjoy!

3½ oz. bittersweet chocolate, finely chopped

7 tablespoons unsalted butter, cut into pieces

2 tablespoons runny honey

3 eggs, separated

½ cup sugar

6 tablespoons all-purpose flour

a pinch of fine sea salt

⅓ cup whole blanched hazelnuts, finely ground

whipped cream, heavy cream, or sweetened crème fraîche, to serve

6 ramekins

Serves 6

Put the chocolate in a microwave-proof bowl and melt in the microwave on HIGH for 40 seconds. Remove, stir, and repeat until almost completely melted. Remove and stir in the butter and honey. Set aside.

Put the egg whites and 1 tablespoon of the sugar in another bowl and beat until firm peaks form. Set aside.

Put the the egg yolks and remaining sugar in a third bowl and beat until slightly thickened and a paler yellow. Using a spatula, fold in the flour and salt. Mix in the nuts. Add one-third of the beaten whites and mix until no streaks of white remain.

Gently fold in the remaining whites, blending well, but taking care not to overmix or you will deflate all the whites.

Preheat the oven to 350°F. Divide the mixture between the ramekins. Set the ramekins on a baking sheet and transfer to the preheated oven. Bake for 12–15 minutes, until just puffed and set but still jiggly in the middle. Serve warm with the cream of your choice.

*NOTE If you don't have a microwave, put the chocolate in a bowl over a saucepan of simmering water—don't let the water touch the bottom of the bowl. Leave until melted, stirring occasionally.

Rhubarb clafoutis

Clafoutis à la rhubarbe

Clafoutis, a custard-like batter baked with whole cherries, is a speciality of the Limousin region. It is one of the finest French desserts and easy to make. The only drawback is that the cherry season is a short one. Plums, pears, and apples work well as substitutes, but rhubarb is fantastic, almost better than the original.

1 lb. fresh rhubarb, cut into 1-inch slices
¾ cup whole milk
¾ cup heavy cream
3 eggs
¾ cup sugar
¼ teaspoon ground cinnamon
a pinch of salt
1 vanilla bean, split lengthwise with
   a small sharp knife
⅓ cup all-purpose flour

*a baking dish, about 12 inches diameter,
   buttered and sprinkled with sugar*

Serves 6

Bring a large saucepan of water to a boil, add the rhubarb, and cook for 2 minutes, just to blanch. Drain and set aside.

Put the milk, cream, eggs, sugar, cinnamon, and salt in a bowl and mix well. Using the tip of the knife, scrape the vanilla seeds into the mixture. Add the flour and whisk well.

Preheat the oven to 400°F. Arrange the rhubarb in the prepared baking dish. Pour the batter over the top and bake in the preheated oven for 40–45 minutes, until puffed and golden.

Tarte tatin Tarte des demoiselles tatin

*An absolute French classic, this is a lot easier to make at home than you might think.
You should invest in the right pan because an ordinary cake or tart pan is not suitable.
Once you make and taste this, you will come back to it time and time again, so the
investment will be more than worthwhile. Crème fraîche is the authentic and best
accompaniment, but simple heavy cream, whipped cream, or even vanilla ice cream
are all perfectly good.*

3½ lbs. apples (about 9), such as
Golden Delicious

1 stick plus 2 tablespoons
unsalted butter

¾ cup sugar

Sweet pastry / Pâte brisée

1½ cups all-purpose flour

2 teaspoons sugar

7 tablespoons cold unsalted butter,
cut into pieces

a pinch of salt

*a tarte tatin pan or other round,
flameproof baking dish (lined
copper or enamelled cast iron
is best)*

Serves 8

To make the pastry, put the flour, sugar, butter, and salt in a food processor
and, using the pulse button, process until the butter is broken down (about
5–10 pulses). Add 3 tablespoons cold water and pulse just until the dough
forms coarse crumbs; add 1 more tablespoon water if necessary, but do not
do more than 10 pulses. Transfer the pastry to a sheet of parchment paper,
form into a ball, and flatten to a disk. Wrap up in the paper and let stand for
30–60 minutes.

Roll out the pastry to a disk the diameter of the pan; turn the pan upside
down on the rolled out pastry, press down and trace around the edge with
the tip of a sharp knife. Transfer the pastry round to a baking sheet and chill
until needed.

Peel, core, and quarter the apples. Set aside.

Put the butter and sugar in the baking pan and melt over high heat, stirring
to blend. Remove from the heat and arrange the apples in the pan in two
circles. The inner circle should go in the opposite direction to the outer one.

Return to the heat and cook for 30 minutes. From this point, watch the
apples carefully, and cook for a further 5–15 minutes, until the liquid thickens
and turns a golden caramel color. Remove from the heat and put the disk of
pastry on top, gently tucking in the edges.

Preheat the oven to 400°F. Transfer the tart to the preheated oven and
bake for 45–60 minutes, until browned . Remove from the oven and let cool
slightly. Invert onto a serving plate while still warm (or the caramel will
harden, making it too difficult). Serve hot, warm, or at room temperature.

Simple apple tart Tarte aux pommes

Golden Delicious is the apple of preference for most French dishes. It's not an especially interesting eating variety, but it's perfect for baking and cooking. It holds its shape well and is not too tart. The vanilla-scented purée is an extra, but well worth the indulgence.

1 recipe Sweet Pastry (see page 140), chilled

Apple purée

3 Golden Delicious apples, peeled and chopped

1 vanilla bean, split lengthwise with a small sharp knife

2 tablespoons sugar

1 tablespoon unsalted butter

Apple topping

3 Golden Delicious apples, peeled and sliced

1 tablespoon unsalted butter, melted

1 tablespoon sugar

parchment paper and baking weights or dried beans

a loose-based tart pan, 11 inches diameter, greased and floured

Serves 6

Roll out the pastry on a floured work surface to a disk slightly larger than the tart pan. Carefully transfer the pastry to the pan, patching any holes as you go and pressing gently into the sides. To trim the edges, roll a rolling pin over the top, using the edge of the pan as a cutting surface, and letting the excess fall away. Tidy up the edges and refrigerate for about 30–60 minutes, until firm.

Preheat the oven to 400°F. Prick the pastry all over, line with parchment paper, and fill with baking weights. Bake in the preheated oven for about 15 minutes, then remove the paper and weights and bake for 10–15 minutes more, until just golden. Let the tart shell cool slightly before filling.

To make the apple purée, put the apples, vanilla bean, sugar, and butter in a saucepan, add 4 tablespoons water and cook gently for about 10–15 minutes, stirring often until soft, adding more water if necessary. Use the tip of the knife to scrape the seeds from the vanilla bean into the purée, then discard the bean. Transfer the mixture to a food processor or blender and purée.

Preheat the oven to 400°F. Spread the purée evenly in the cooled tart shell. Arrange the apple slices in a circle around the edge; they should be slightly overlapping but not completely squashed together. Repeat for an inner circle, trimming the slices slightly so they fit, and going in the opposite direction to the outer circle.

Brush with melted butter and sprinkle with sugar. Bake in the preheated oven for about 25–35 minutes, until browned and the apples are tender. Serve warm or at room temperature.

Pear and almond tart

Tarte aux poires frangipane

This is very elegant, both in appearance and flavor. It is ideal for entertaining since the tart shell and almond cream can be made a few hours in advance. To make it even more special, serve with crème fraîche sweetened with a little sugar, or good quality vanilla ice cream.

1 pre-baked Sweet Pastry tart shell, still in its pan and cooled (see page 142)

3–4 ripe pears*

Almond cream

7 tablespoons unsalted butter

½ cup sugar

2 eggs

½ cup ground almonds, or slivered almonds ground to a powder

2 tablespoons all-purpose flour

parchment paper and baking weights or dried beans

a loose-based tart pan, 11 inches diameter, greased and floured

Serves 6

To make the almond cream, put the butter and sugar in a bowl and beat with an electric mixer until fluffy and lemon-colored. Beat in the eggs, one at a time. Using a spatula, fold in the almonds and flour until well mixed.

Preheat the oven to 375°F.

Spread the almond cream evenly in the tart shell.

Peel and slice the pears, into 8 or 12 slices, depending on the size of the pears. Arrange the pear slices on top of the almond cream.

Bake in the preheated oven for about 20–25 minutes, until puffed and golden. Serve warm.

*NOTE If only unripe pears are available, poach them for 5 minutes in a saucepan of water with the freshly squeezed juice of ½ a lemon

Fresh fruit tart Tarte aux fruits frais

In French pastry shops, this tart is often made in a more orderly fashion, with all the fruit arranged in neat circles. I find it is prettier—and more accessible for the home cook—to use the higgledy-piggledy approach to fruit distribution. You can pile it as high as you like, but be warned that it can get a bit messy when serving. This does not in any way affect the taste.

1 pre-baked Sweet Pastry tart shell, still in its pan and cooled (see page 142)

Pastry cream

2 cups whole milk
(or half milk and half cream)

1 vanilla bean, split lengthwise with a small sharp knife

5 egg yolks

¼ cup sugar

⅓ cup all-purpose flour

Fruit filling

1 small basket blackberries

1 small baket blueberries

1 small basket strawberries

1 peach, thinly sliced

1 nectarine, thinly sliced

2 purple plums, thinly sliced

1 kiwi fruit, peeled, halved and thinly sliced

about ½ cup apricot preserve

parchment paper and baking weights or dried beans

a loose-based tart pan, 11 inches diameter, greased and floured

Serves 8–10

To make the pasry cream put the milk and vanilla bean in a heavy saucepan and bring just to a boil. Remove from the heat, cover and leave to infuse for 15 minutes.

Put the egg yolks and sugar in a heatproof bowl and whisk well. Add the flour and mix well. Strain the milk into the yolk mixture and whisk until smooth. Return to the saucepan and continue cooking over low heat for 2 minutes, stirring constantly. It will thicken. Transfer to a shallow bowl to cool. (This can be prepared up to 1 day in advance if covered and refrigerated.)

Spread the pastry cream in an even layer in the cooled tart shell. Arrange the fruit on top. I start with one kind, using almost all of it, and then go on to another, until I've used all the types. Then I go back and fill in the holes with the remaining pieces.

Melt the preserve and 2 tablespoons water in a small saucepan set over low heat. Strain to remove all the lumpy bits. Using a pastry brush, carefully but generously dab or brush the preserve over the fruit to form a shiny glaze. Let cool. Refrigerate 6–8 hours in advance, but return to almost room temperature to serve.

*VARIATION For a fresh strawberry tart, use 2–3 large baskets of washed and dried strawberries, halved and/or sliced depending on size. Glaze with redcurrant jelly instead of apricot preserve—it shouldn't need straining.

Baked fruit and custard tart

Tarte aux fruits alsacienne

Almost any fruit can be used for this recipe, which is Alsatian in origin. Plums are especially nice and any variety will do; it's even nicer if you mix yellow and purple plums. Whatever fruit you choose, the amount does depend on the size, but use the weight as a rough guide and allow a bit more, just in case. Try this with peaches, apricots, nectarines, rhubarb, or apples too.

1 pre-baked Sweet Pastry tart shell,
   still in its pan (see page 142),
   (baked in a round or
   rectangular pan) and cooled

Tart filling

1½–2 lbs. plums, just ripe but not
   too soft

2 eggs

6 tablespoons heavy cream

6 tablespoons sugar, plus more
   for sprinkling

Serves 6

To make the filling, quarter the plums and remove the pits. Arrange the plums
in the tart shell in two circles if using a round tart pan, or in lines if using
a rectangular pan. If using a round pan, the inner circle should go in the
opposite direction from the outer one.

Preheat the oven to 400°F.

Put the eggs, cream, and sugar in a large bowl and beat well. Set the tart
shell carefully on a baking sheet and pour the egg mixture over the fruit,
taking care to fill the tart evenly.

Transfer to the preheated oven and bake for 35–45 minues, until puffed,
just set and beginning to turn golden brown.

Remove from the oven. Sprinkle generously with sugar and serve warm or
at room temperature.

I must have made a thousand lemon tarts in my day, but I really struggled to get this good enough to publish. The key lessons learned from my mistakes are these. The oven temperature must not be too high or the mixture will curdle unattractively. You really must fill the tart shell on the pulled-out oven shelf; it should be filled right to the top and no one could possibly transfer from counter to oven without spilling. And try not to do too many other things whilst baking.

Lemon tart Tarte au citron

1 pre-baked Sweet Pastry tart shell, still in its pan and cooled (see page 142)

confectioners' sugar, to dust

Lemon filling

3 lemons

½ an orange

1 cup sugar

3 whole eggs and 2 egg yolks

scant 1 cup heavy cream

parchment paper and baking weights or dried beans

a loose-based tart pan, 11 inches diameter, greased and floured

Serves 10

Preheat the oven to 300°F.

To make the filling, squeeze the juice from the lemons and the orange half and strain into a bowl.

Add the sugar, eggs, and egg yolks to the bowl and whisk just enough to blend in the eggs. Do not whisk too vigorously or the mixture will be too frothy. Stir in the cream.

Put the cooled tart shell on a baking sheet and set this on the oven rack, partly pulled out. Pour the lemon mixture through a strainer directly into the tart shell and carefully slide the oven shelf back into place. Alternatively, strain the mixture into a pitcher, then pour it into the tart shell before sliding the shelf into the oven. Bake in the preheated oven for 20–25 minutes, until just set. Let cool.

Dust with confectioners' sugar and serve immediately, at room temperature.

A very simple and elegant tart recipe. The chestnut flavor is subtle but quite pleasant, and it makes the texture much creamier and smoother. This can easily be made in advance and kept in the refrigerator until needed (for up to 24 hours), but do not serve it chilled; room temperature is ideal.

Chocolate chestnut tart Tarte au chocolat et aux marrons

1 pre-baked Sweet Pastry tart shell, still in its pan and cooled (see page 142)

unsweetened cocoa powder, for dusting

whipped cream or sweetened crème fraîche, to serve

Chocolate chestnut filling

4 oz. bittersweet chocolate, finely chopped

3 tablespoons unsalted butter

1 extra-large egg, beaten

¾ cup heavy cream

1 cup canned sweetened chestnut purée

parchment paper and baking weights or dried beans

a loose-based tart pan, 11 inches diameter, greased and floured

Preheat the oven to 300°F.

To make the filling, put the chocolate in a large microwave-proof bowl and microwave on HIGH for 30 seconds. Remove, stir, and repeat until almost completely melted. Remove, add the butter and stir until melted.

Stir in the egg, cream, and chestnut purée and mix just to blend.

Put the tart shell on a baking sheet and set this on the oven rack, partly pulled out. (If you try to fill the shell and then transfer it to the oven, it will surely spill over the edges and burn.) Pour the chocolate mixture into the tart shell and carefully slide the oven shelf back into place.

Bake in the preheated oven for 20–25 minutes, until just set. Let cool to room temperature before serving.

*NOTE If you don't have a microwave, put the chocolate in a bowl over a saucepan of simmering water—don't let the water touch the bottom of the bowl. Leave until melted, stirring occasionally.

Serves 8–10

Walnut cake Gâteau aux noix

Walnuts figure prominently in the cuisine of the south-west, though I would say this is a traditional all-over-France sort of dessert. It is formal and elegant, but not too fussy. Just the right thing to finish off a Sunday lunch. It is equally nice with a cup of tea and some friendly afternoon chat. This cake keeps well, too, so you can make it a day or two in advance.

1 stick plus 6 tablespoons unsalted butter, softened

1 cup sugar

1 vanilla bean, split lengthwise with a small sharp knife

4 extra-large eggs

1½ cups all-purpose flour

1 cup walnuts pieces, ground

walnut halves, to decorate

Caramel frosting

½ cup sugar

a squeeze of fresh lemon juice

⅔ cup heavy cream

a cake pan, 9 inches diameter, greased

Serves 6-8

Preheat the oven to 400°F.

Put the butter and sugar in a large bowl and beat until fluffy. Use the tip of the knife to scrape in the vanilla seeds. Add the eggs one at a time, beating well after each addition. Using a spatula, gently fold in the flour and ground walnuts. Transfer to the prepared cake pan.

Bake in the preheated oven for 25–35 minutes, until browned and a knife inserted in the middle comes out clean. Let cool slightly, then unmold while still warm.

To make the caramel frosting, put the sugar, lemon juice, and 3 tablespoons water in a heavy saucepan and cook, stirring, until it turns a light caramel color. Carefully add the cream (it can splatter), stirring until blended.

Put the cake on a wire rack set over a baking sheet to catch the drips. Pour over the frosting in a thin, even layer. Decorate with walnut halves and leave for at least 2–3 hours before slicing, until the frosting has set.

This traditional recipe is simplicity itself to bake. The ½-cup yogurt pot is the measure, so it doesn't really matter what size—or flavor—you use, but plain, set yogurt is my preference. If you don't fancy the orange, try other flavorings: cinnamon, honey, vanilla, chocolate, fresh or dried fruit pieces—all work very well. This is great fun to make with children.

Yogurt cake   Gâteau au yaourt

½ cup plain set yogurt

1 cup sugar

1½ cups flour

2 eggs

1 tablespoon safflower oil

1 teaspoon baking soda

a pinch of salt

freshly squeezed juice of 1 orange

1 tablespoon confectioners' sugar, to decorate

a deep-sided cake pan, 9 inches diameter, greased

Serves 8

Preheat the oven to 350°F.

Empty the yogurt into a large bowl and wipe out the pot so when you measure the other ingredients, they won't stick. Otherwise, just use regular measuring cups. Add the sugar, flour, eggs, oil, baking soda, salt, and half the orange juice. Stir well.

Pour into the prepared cake pan and bake in the preheated oven for 15–20 minutes, until a knife inserted in the middle comes out clean. Remove from the oven and pierce a few holes in the top with a fork. Pour over the remaining orange juice. Let cool slightly, then turn out onto a wire rack to cool.

To decorate, put the confectioners' sugar in a strainer and hold it over the cake. Tap the edge of the strainer to release the sugar, moving around the surface to coat. A very light dusting is sufficient. Serve at room temperature.

Index

conversion chart

Weights and measures have been rounded up or down slightly to make measuring easier.

Measuring butter:

A US stick of butter weighs 4 oz. which is approximately 115 g or 8 level tablespoons. The recipes in this book require the following conversions:

American	Metric	Imperial
6 tbsp	85 g	3 oz.
7 tbsp	100 g	3½ oz.
1 stick	115 g	4 oz.

Volume equivalents:

1 teaspoon	5 ml
1 tablespoon	15 ml

American	Metric	Imperial
¼ cup	60 ml	2 fl. oz.
⅓ cup	75 ml	2½ fl. oz.
½ cup	125 ml	4 fl. oz.
⅔ cup	150 ml	5 fl. oz. (¼ pint)
¾ cup	175 ml	6 fl. oz.
1 cup	250 ml	8 fl. oz.

Weight equivalents: / Measurements:

Imperial	Metric	Inches	cm
1 oz.	30 g	¼ inch	5 mm
2 oz.	55 g	½ inch	1 cm
3 oz.	85 g	1 inch	2.5 cm
3½ oz.	100 g	2 inches	5 cm
4 oz.	115 g	3 inches	7 cm
6 oz.	175 g	4 inches	10 cm
8 oz. (½ lb.)	225 g	5 inches	12 cm
9 oz.	250 g	6 inches	15 cm
10 oz.	280 g	7 inches	18 cm
12 oz.	350 g	8 inches	20 cm
13 oz.	375 g	9 inches	23 cm
14 oz.	400 g	10 inches	25 cm
15 oz.	425 g	11 inches	28 cm
16 oz. (1 lb.)	450 g	12 inches	30 cm

Oven temperatures:

120°C	(250°F)	Gas ½
140°C	(275°F)	Gas 1
150°C	(300°F)	Gas 2
170°C	(325°F)	Gas 3
180°C	(350°F)	Gas 4
190°C	(375°F)	Gas 5
200°C	(400°F)	Gas 6
220°C	(425°F)	Gas 7

Photography credits

Key: a=above, b=below, r=right, l=left, c=center.

Martin Brigdale
Endpapers, pages 10, 11, 13, 14, 16, 17, 18, 22, 23, 25, 26, 29, 32, 36, 39, 41–46, 49, 50, 53, 54, 57, 61, 63, 64, 67, 68, 70, 72, 74, 76, 77, 78, 80, 81 inset, 82, 83, 84, 89, 90, 92, 95, 96, 98, 100, 102, 105, 107, 109, 111al, 111br, 112r, 113, 114, 116, 119, 122a, 123, 124, 128–137, 139, 141, 143, 145, 147, 149, 150, 152, 155, 156, 160

Peter Cassidy
Pages 3, 15, 24, 27, 30, 40, 48, 56 both, 65 both, 66, 85, 88, 106, 111ar, 111bl, 112l, 117, 120, 125, 126, 127, 140, 153: Pages 2, 8, 108, 122b La Mas del la Rose, designed by Enrica Stabile (www.utile-dilettevole.it), available to rent through www.theluberon.com/masdelarose.htm

Christopher Drake
Pages 34: Florence and Pierre Pallardy, Domaine de la Baronnie, Saint-Martin de Ré (www.labaronnie-pallardy.com); 51, 58: interior designer Carole Oulhen (+ 33 6 80 99 66 16); 71: family home near Aix-en-Provence with interior design by Daisy Simon (daisy.simonaix@wanadoo.fr); 115: Mireille and Jean Claude Lothon, La Cour Beaudeval Antiquities, 4 rue des Fontaines, 28210 Faverolles (+ 33 2 37 51 47 67); 144, 148 the Chateau de Gignac, Gignac en Provence 84400 France www.gaspard-degignac.com; 157 Annie-Camille Kuentzmann-Levet Décoration (+ 33 1 30 42 53 59)

Richard Jung
Pages 31, 91, 138

Paul Massey
Page 79: Cote Jardin boutique (Place du Marche, 17590 Ars En Re, France)

© Steve Painter
Pages 1, 4, 5, 6, 7, 9, 21, 35, 59, 75, 81 background, 87, 93, 99, 103, 118, 121

Claire Richardson
Pages 104: Richard Goullet, décorateur (www.richardgoullet-decoration.com, richardgoullet@gmail.com); 151: Josephine Ryan Antiques (www.josephineryanantiques.co.uk)

Fritz von der Schulenburg
Page 60: Irene & Giorgio Silvagni's house in Provence

Yuki Sugiura
Page 20

Kate Whitaker
Pages 12, 28

Polly Wreford
Page 86: the home of stylist Twig Hutchinson in London (www.twighutchinson.com)